coffee
100 everyday recipes

First published in 2012
LOVE FOOD is an imprint of Parragon Books Ltd

Parragon
Queen Street House
4 Queen Street
Bath BA1 1HE, UK

Copyright © Parragon Books Ltd 2012

LOVE FOOD and the accompanying heart device is a registered trade mark of Parragon Books Ltd in Australia, the UK, USA, India and the EU.

www.parragon.com/lovefood

ISBN: 978-1-4454-9872-0

Printed in China

Produced by Ivy Contract
Cover and new internal photography by Clive Streeter
Cover and new home economy by Angela Drake

Notes for the Reader

This book uses both metric and imperial measurements. Follow the same units of measurement throughout; do not mix metric and imperial. All spoon measurements are level: teaspoons are assumed to be 5 ml, and tablespoons are assumed to be 15 ml. Unless otherwise stated, milk is assumed to be full fat, eggs and individual vegetables are medium, and pepper is freshly ground black pepper. Unless otherwise stated, all root vegetables should be washed in plain water and peeled prior to using.

For best results, use a food thermometer when cooking meat and poultry – check the latest government guidelines for current advice. Garnishes, decorations and serving suggestions are all optional and not necessarily included in the recipe ingredients or method.

The times given are an approximate guide only. Preparation times differ according to the techniques used by different people and the cooking times may also vary from those given. Optional ingredients, variations or serving suggestions have not been included in the time calculations.

Recipes using raw or very lightly cooked eggs should be avoided by infants, the elderly, pregnant women, convalescents and anyone suffering from an illness. Pregnant and breastfeeding women are advised to avoid eating peanuts and peanut products. Sufferers from nut allergies should be aware that some of the ready-made ingredients used in the recipes in this book may contain nuts. Always check the packaging before use.

In recipes that call for black coffee or strong black coffee, cafetiere or instant coffee should be used and made up with hot water to taste.

coffee

introduction

Coffee is so much more than just a drink to jump-start your day. This much-loved stimulant is a universal favourite in cooking, and tastes as good in simple recipes as it does in more complex, luxurious ones. Coffee has an intense, heady aroma and adds a nuttiness and rich, fabulous flavour to whatever you're cooking. Think of coffee as a versatile spice that can be used to season a whole range of delectable recipes, from savoury to sweet.

This book celebrates the numerous creative ways that coffee can be used in the kitchen. Chapters cover small cakes and biscuits, family cakes, desserts, savoury recipes and drinks. Here you'll find an irresistible collection of tried and tested coffee recipes, from classic cakes to scrumptious sweet treats. Coffee can bring out the flavours of meats without imparting an overwhelming taste of coffee. It is also a natural in many drinks and cocktails, though you might want to use decaffeinated later in the evening!

These recipes use all types of coffee: brewed coffee, coffee and chicory essence, powder, granules and coffee-flavoured liqueurs. For best results and maximum indulgence you should choose top-quality coffee to create a perfect dish every time. Refrigerate freshly ground coffee in an airtight container and use quickly since it begins to lose its flavour after a couple of days. Keep whole roasted beans in an airtight container in a cool, dry place for up to two weeks, or for up to three months in a freezer. You can also freeze leftover coffee in ice trays to use at a later date, in iced coffee or stews, for example.

When consumed in moderation, coffee has many health benefits and is full of antioxidants. It may also reduce the risk of developing type-2 diabetes, certain types of cancer, cirrhosis and gallstones. So now that you know coffee can be a health food too, you'll find plenty of ideas in this book to use and enjoy it whatever the time of day.

small cakes, bars & biscuits

mini coffee & maple bundt cakes

ingredients

makes 4

115 g/4 oz butter, softened,
  plus extra for greasing
115 g/4 oz caster sugar
2 eggs, beaten
175 g/6 oz self-raising flour,
  sifted, plus extra for dusting
1 tbsp coffee and chicory essence
4 tbsp buttermilk

icing

115 g/4 oz icing sugar
2 tbsp maple syrup
1–2 tsp water

method

1 Preheat the oven to 180°C/350°F/Gas Mark 4.
  Thoroughly grease 4 x 200-ml/7-fl oz bundt tins, then
  dust each with a little flour, tipping out any excess.

2 Put the butter and sugar into a bowl and beat together
  until pale and creamy. Gradually beat in the eggs,
  then fold in half the flour. Fold in the coffee and
  chicory essence and buttermilk, followed by the
  remaining flour.

3 Divide the mixture between the prepared tins. Place on
  a baking sheet and bake in the preheated oven for
  25–30 minutes, or until risen and firm to the touch.
  Cool in the tins for 5 minutes, then turn out onto a wire
  rack and leave to cool completely.

4 To make the icing, sift the sugar into a bowl and stir in
  the maple syrup and water, then mix until smooth.
  Drizzle over the cakes and leave to set.

coffee & almond cakes

ingredients

makes 6

115 g/4 oz self-raising flour

¼ tsp baking powder

115 g/4 oz soft light brown sugar

115 g/4 oz butter, softened,
plus extra for greasing

2 eggs, beaten

25 g/1 oz ground almonds

2 tsp instant coffee granules,
dissolved in 2 tbsp hot milk

2 tbsp flaked almonds, toasted,
to decorate

buttercream

85 g/3 oz butter, softened

175 g/6 oz icing sugar

2 tsp coffee and chicory essence

method

1 Preheat the oven to 180°C/350°F/Gas Mark 4. Grease
6 x 175-ml/6-fl oz mini loaf tins and base-line with
baking paper.

2 Sift together the flour and baking powder into a bowl
and add the sugar, butter, eggs and ground almonds.
Beat with an electric whisk for 2–3 minutes, until
smooth and creamy. Whisk in the dissolved coffee.

3 Divide the mixture between the prepared tins,
smoothing the surfaces with a small palette knife. Place
the tins on a baking sheet and bake the cakes in the
preheated oven for 20–25 minutes, or until risen,
golden and just firm to the touch. Leave in the tins for
5 minutes, then carefully turn out onto a wire rack and
leave to cool completely.

4 To make the buttercream, put the butter into a bowl
and gradually beat in the sugar, then beat in the coffee
and chicory essence until smooth. Spread the
buttercream over the cakes and sprinkle with the
flaked almonds.

coffee & pecan streusel muffins

ingredients

makes 12

250 g/9 oz plain flour
1 tbsp baking powder
55 g/2 oz pecan nuts, finely
    chopped
115 g/4 oz caster sugar
85 g/3 oz butter,
    chilled and coarsely grated
1 large egg, beaten
125 ml/4 fl oz milk
4 tbsp strong black coffee, cooled

streusel topping

40 g/1½ oz plain flour
25 g/1 oz butter
25 g/1 oz pecan nuts, chopped
1½ tsp instant coffee granules,
    finely ground
25 g/1 oz demerara sugar

method

1 Preheat the oven to 200°C/400°F/Gas Mark 6. Line a 12-hole muffin tin with 12 paper muffin cases.

2 Sift together the flour and baking powder into a large bowl and stir in the nuts and sugar. Add the butter and stir with a fork to coat in the flour mixture.

3 Beat together the egg, milk and coffee and stir into the dry ingredients. Mix lightly until just combined, taking care not to overbeat. Divide the mixture between the muffin cases.

4 To make the topping, put the flour in a bowl and rub in the butter to make fine crumbs. Stir in the nuts, coffee and sugar. Sprinkle the streusel topping evenly over the muffins.

5 Bake in the preheated oven for 20–25 minutes, or until risen, golden and just firm to the touch. Cool for 5 minutes, then transfer to a wire rack and leave to cool completely.

irish coffee muffins

ingredients

makes 12

1 tbsp sunflower or groundnut oil,
    for brushing (if using)
280 g/10 oz plain flour
1 tbsp baking powder
pinch of salt
85 g/3 oz butter
55 g/2 oz demerara sugar
1 large egg, beaten
125 ml/4 fl oz double cream
1 tsp almond extract
2 tbsp strong black coffee, cooled
2 tbsp coffee-flavoured liqueur
4 tbsp Irish whiskey
whipped double cream,
    to serve (optional)

method

1 Preheat the oven to 200°C/400°F/Gas Mark 6. Brush a 12-hole muffin tin with sunflower oil, or line it with 12 paper muffin cases. Sift the flour, baking powder and salt into a large mixing bowl.

2 In a separate large bowl, cream the butter and sugar together, then stir in the beaten egg. Pour in the double cream, almond extract, coffee, liqueur and whiskey and stir together. Add the whiskey mixture to the flour mixture and then gently stir together until just combined. Do not overstir the mixture – it is fine for it to be a little lumpy.

3 Divide the muffin mixture evenly between the 12 holes in the muffin tin or the paper cases (they should be about two-thirds full). Bake in the preheated oven for 20 minutes, or until risen and golden. Remove the muffins from the oven and serve warm, or place them on a wire rack to cool. If liked, fill the muffins with whipped double cream, to serve.

after-dinner coffee liqueur muffins

ingredients

makes 12

oil or melted butter,
    for greasing
2 tbsp instant coffee granules
2 tbsp boiling water
280 g/10 oz plain flour
1 tbsp baking powder
pinch of salt
115 g/4 oz soft light brown sugar
2 eggs
100 ml/3½ fl oz milk
85 g/3 oz butter, melted and
    cooled
6 tbsp coffee liqueur
40 g/1½ oz demerara sugar

method

1 Preheat the oven to 200°C/400°F/Gas Mark 6. Grease a 12-hole muffin tin or line with 12 paper muffin cases. Put the coffee granules and boiling water in a cup and stir until dissolved. Leave to cool.

2 Meanwhile, sift together the flour, baking powder and salt into a large bowl. Stir in the brown sugar.

3 Lightly beat the eggs in a large bowl then beat in the milk, butter, dissolved coffee and liqueur. Make a well in the centre of the dry ingredients and pour in the beaten liquid ingredients. Stir gently until just combined; do not over-mix.

4 Spoon the mixture into the prepared muffin tin or paper cases. Sprinkle the demerara sugar over the tops of the muffins. Bake in the preheated oven for about 20 minutes until well risen, golden brown and firm to the touch.

5 Leave the muffins in the tin for 5 minutes then serve warm or transfer to a wire rack and leave to cool.

marbled coffee muffins

ingredients

makes 12

280 g/10 oz plain flour
1 tbsp baking powder
pinch of salt
115 g/4 oz caster sugar
2 eggs
250 ml/9 fl oz milk
6 tbsp sunflower oil or 85 g/3 oz
    butter, melted and cooled,
    plus extra for greasing
1 tsp vanilla extract
2 tbsp espresso coffee powder

method

1 Preheat the oven to 200°C/400°F/Gas Mark 6. Grease a 12-hole muffin tin. Sift together the flour, baking powder and salt into a large bowl. Stir in the sugar.

2 Put the eggs in a large jug or bowl and beat lightly, then beat in the milk, oil and vanilla extract. Make a well in the centre of the dry ingredients and pour in the beaten liquid ingredients. Stir gently until just combined; do not overmix.

3 Divide the mixture between two bowls. Sift the coffee powder into one bowl and mix together. Using teaspoons, spoon the mixtures into the muffin tin, alternating the coffee mixture and the plain mixture.

4 Bake in the preheated oven for 20 minutes, or until well risen, golden brown and firm to the touch. Leave to cool in the tin for 5 minutes, then serve warm or transfer to a wire rack to cool completely.

coffee fudge cupcakes

ingredients

makes 28

175 g/6 oz plain white flour
1 tbsp baking powder
175 g/6 oz unsalted butter,
    softened
175 g/6 oz caster sugar
3 eggs, beaten
1 tsp coffee extract
2 tbsp milk
chocolate-covered coffee beans,
    to decorate

frosting

55 g/2 oz unsalted butter
115 g/4 oz light muscovado sugar
2 tbsp single cream or milk
½ tsp coffee extract
400 g/14 oz icing sugar, sifted

method

1 Preheat the oven to 190°C/375°F/Gas Mark 5. Place 28 paper cases into bun tins or put 28 double-layer paper cases onto baking trays.

2 Sift the flour and baking powder into a large bowl and add the butter, caster sugar, eggs and coffee extract. Beat well until the mixture is smooth, then beat in the milk.

3 Divide the mixture between the paper cases. Bake in the preheated oven for 15–20 minutes, or until risen, firm and golden brown. Transfer the cupcakes to a wire rack to cool.

4 To make the frosting, place the butter, muscovado sugar, cream and coffee extract in a saucepan over a medium heat and stir until melted and smooth. Bring to the boil and boil, stirring, for 2 minutes. Remove from the heat and beat in the icing sugar.

5 Stir the frosting until smooth and thick, then spoon into a piping bag fitted with a large star nozzle. Pipe a swirl of frosting on top of each cupcake and top with a coffee bean.

feather-iced coffee cupcakes

ingredients

makes 16

1 tbsp instant coffee granules
1 tbsp boiling water
115 g/4 oz butter, softened,
    or soft margarine
100 g/3½ oz soft
    light brown sugar
2 eggs
100 g/3½ oz self-raising flour
½ tsp baking powder
2 tbsp soured cream

icing

225 g/8 oz icing sugar
4 tsp warm water
1 tsp instant coffee granules
2 tsp boiling water

method

1 Preheat the oven to 190°C/375°F/Gas Mark 5. Line two 12-hole muffin tins with 16 paper cases. Put the coffee granules in a cup or small bowl, add the boiling water and stir until dissolved. Cool slightly.

2 Put the butter, sugar and eggs in a large bowl. Sift in the flour and baking powder and beat until smooth. Add the dissolved coffee and soured cream and beat until mixed. Spoon the mixture into the paper cases.

3 Bake in the preheated oven for 20 minutes, or until well risen and golden. Cool on a wire rack.

4 To make the icing, sift 90 g/3¼ oz of the icing sugar into a bowl and add enough warm water to mix until thick enough to coat the back of a wooden spoon. Dissolve the coffee in the boiling water. Sift the remaining icing sugar into a bowl and stir in the dissolved coffee. Ice the cakes with the white icing, then pipe the coffee icing in parallel lines on top. Draw a skewer across the piped lines in both directions. Leave to set before serving.

mocha cherry buns

ingredients

makes 12

85 g/3 oz plain chocolate, broken
    into pieces
150 g/5½ oz self-raising flour
1 tbsp cocoa powder
1½ tbsp instant coffee powder
2 eggs, lightly beaten
55 g/2 oz butter, softened
3 tbsp milk
115 g/4 oz soft light brown sugar
24 fresh cherries, stoned
icing sugar, for dusting

method

1 Preheat the oven to 180°C/350°F/Gas Mark 4. Line a 12-hole muffin tin with paper muffin cases.

2 Put the chocolate in a heatproof bowl, set the bowl over a saucepan of gently simmering water and heat until melted. Leave to cool for 5 minutes.

3 Sift together the flour and cocoa powder into a bowl and add the coffee powder, eggs, butter, milk and brown sugar. Beat with an electric whisk for 2–3 minutes, until smooth. Fold in the melted chocolate.

4 Spoon the mixture into the paper cases. Top each bun with two cherries. Bake in the preheated oven for 20–25 minutes, or until risen and firm to the touch. Transfer to a wire rack and leave to cool. Dust with icing sugar just before serving.

coffee crumb cakes

ingredients

makes 18

topping

85 g/3 oz plain flour
70 g/2½ oz lightly salted butter, cut into pieces
½ tsp ground mixed spice
1½ tsp ground espresso coffee
70 g/2½ oz caster sugar

sponge

55 g/2 oz lightly salted butter, softened, plus extra for greasing
100 g/3½ oz caster sugar
1 egg
5 tbsp soured cream
125 g/4½ oz self-raising flour, sifted

icing

85 g/3 oz icing sugar, sifted
1 tbsp strong espresso coffee, cooled

method

1 Preheat the oven to 180°C/350°F/Gas Mark 4. Grease a 20-cm/8-inch square, shallow cake tin and line with baking paper.

2 To make the topping, put the plain flour, butter, mixed spice and coffee in a food processor or blender and process until the mixture starts to resemble coarse breadcrumbs. Add the caster sugar and process again briefly. Tip the mixture into a mixing bowl.

3 To make the sponge, put the butter, caster sugar, egg, soured cream and self-raising flour in the food processor or blender and process until smooth and creamy. Turn out into the tin and smooth level with a palette knife. Sprinkle the topping in an even layer on top. Bake in the preheated oven for 30–35 minutes, or until risen and firm to the touch and a skewer inserted into the centre comes out clean. Leave in the tin for 10 minutes, then transfer to a wire rack to cool.

4 To make the icing, put all but 2 tablespoons of the icing sugar in a small mixing bowl and add the coffee. Beat to a smooth paste that falls in a thick trail from the spoon, adding a little more icing sugar if necessary. Cut the cake into three even-sized pieces, then cut across to make 18 rectangular pieces. Drizzle with the icing.

mocha raspberry crumble bars

ingredients

makes 8

175 g/6 oz butter, softened,
  plus extra for greasing
250 g/9 oz plain flour, sifted
1½ tbsp instant coffee powder
85 g/3 oz caster sugar
5 tbsp raspberry jam
40 g/1½ oz chopped mixed nuts
2 tbsp demerara sugar

method

1 Preheat the oven to 180°C/350°F/Gas Mark 4. Grease a 20-cm/8-inch square, shallow cake tin and line with baking paper.

2 Put the butter, flour, coffee powder and caster sugar into a food processor or blender and process for a few seconds, until the mixture starts to clump together.

3 Press three-quarters of the shortbread mixture into the base of the prepared tin in an even layer. Pat down to make it smooth.

4 Bake in the preheated oven for 20 minutes, or until pale golden in colour. Remove from the oven and leave to cool for 5 minutes. Spread the jam over the base. Mix the nuts and demerara sugar into the remaining shortbread mixture and scatter this over the jam, pressing down gently.

5 Return to the oven for a further 20–25 minutes, or until the topping is golden brown. Leave in the tin to cool completely, then remove and cut into eight bars.

variation

Replace the raspberry jam with apricot or blueberry jam.

cinnamon coffee rolls

ingredients

makes 9

450 g/1 lb strong white flour,
    plus extra for dusting
¼ tsp salt
1½ tsp easy-blend dried yeast
40 g/1½ oz caster sugar
55 g/2 oz butter, melted, plus extra
    for greasing
1 egg, beaten
200 ml/7 fl oz lukewarm milk
oil, for greasing
115 g/4 oz icing sugar, mixed to a
    smooth icing with 3–4 tsp
    water, to decorate

filling

40 g/1½ oz butter, softened
50 g/1¾ oz soft dark brown sugar
1½ tsp instant coffee granules,
    finely ground
1 tsp ground cinnamon

method

1 Sift together the flour and salt into a large bowl. Stir in the yeast and sugar and make a well in the centre. Beat together the butter, egg and milk in a jug, then pour into the well and mix to a soft dough. Turn out the dough onto a lightly floured surface and knead for 5–6 minutes, until smooth and elastic, adding more flour if it is too sticky. Place the dough in a bowl, cover with lightly oiled clingfilm and leave in a warm place for 1½ hours, or until doubled in size. Grease a 23-cm/9-inch square cake tin.

2 Turn out the dough onto a floured surface and lightly knead for 1 minute. Roll out to a 30-cm/12-inch square. To make the filling, spread the butter over the dough. Mix together the sugar, coffee and cinnamon and scatter over the butter in an even layer. Roll up the dough from one side. Using a sharp knife cut into nine rounds and place the rolls cut-side up in the prepared tin. Cover loosely with oiled clingfilm and leave for 40–50 minutes, or until doubled in size. Meanwhile, preheat the oven to 200°C/400°F/Gas Mark 6.

3 Bake the rolls in the preheated oven for 18–20 minutes, or until risen and golden. Leave in the tin for 10 minutes, then turn out onto a wire rack and leave to cool.

4 Drizzle the icing over the rolls, leave to set, then pull apart to serve.

coffee caramel éclairs

ingredients

makes 12

choux pastry

150 ml/5 fl oz water
55 g/2 oz butter,
    plus extra for greasing
70 g/2½ oz plain flour, sifted
2 eggs, lightly beaten

filling

300 ml/10 fl oz double cream
4 tbsp rum
1 tbsp icing sugar

coffee caramel

200 g/7 oz sugar
8 tbsp water
1 tsp instant coffee

method

1 Put the water and butter in a saucepan and heat gently until the butter melts, then turn up the heat and bring it rapidly to the boil. Immediately add all the flour, remove the pan from the heat and stir the mixture into a paste that leaves the sides of the pan clean.

2 Meanwhile, preheat the oven to 220°C/425°F/Gas Mark 7. Grease a baking sheet and prepare a piping bag fitted with a plain 2-cm/¾-inch nozzle. Gradually beat the eggs into the flour paste and continue beating until it is smooth and glossy. Spoon the paste into the bag and pipe 12 strips of paste on the baking sheet.

3 Bake for 15 minutes. Reduce the oven temperature to 190°C/375°F/Gas Mark 5 and cook for a further 20–25 minutes, until the éclairs are risen, browned and crisp. Transfer to a wire rack, slitting each pastry lengthways along the side to allow steam to escape. Leave to cool.

4 Whip the cream with the rum and icing sugar. Pipe into the pastries and return them to the wire rack, placing it over a baking sheet. Keep the pastries close together.

5 Put the sugar in a pan and add the water. Heat gently until the sugar has dissolved. Bring to the boil and boil rapidly, without stirring, until the syrup turns golden. Remove from the heat and stir in the coffee using a metal fork. Drizzle over the éclairs. Leave to set and cool.

cappuccino squares

ingredients

makes 15

225 g/8 oz self-raising flour
1 tsp baking powder
1 tsp cocoa powder, plus extra
    for dusting
225 g/8 oz butter, softened,
    plus extra for greasing
225 g/8 oz caster sugar
4 eggs, beaten
3 tbsp instant coffee powder,
    dissolved in 2 tbsp hot water

white chocolate frosting

115 g/4 oz white chocolate,
    broken into pieces
55 g/2 oz butter, softened
3 tbsp milk
175 g/6 oz icing sugar

method

1 Preheat the oven to 180°C/350°F/Gas Mark 4. Lightly grease and base-line a shallow 28 x 18-cm/11 x 7-inch cake tin.

2 Sift the flour, baking powder and cocoa into a bowl and add the butter, caster sugar, eggs and coffee. Beat well by hand or using an electric whisk, until smooth, then spoon the mixture into the prepared tin and smooth the surface with a palette knife.

3 Bake in the preheated oven for 35–40 minutes, or until risen and firm to the touch, then turn out onto a wire rack, and cool completely.

4 To make the frosting, place the chocolate, butter and milk in a heatproof bowl set over a saucepan of simmering water and stir until the chocolate has melted. Remove the bowl from the pan and sift in the icing sugar. Beat until smooth, then spread over the cake. Dust the top of the cake with sifted cocoa, then cut into squares.

variation

To make a coffee frosting, substitute 2–3 teaspoons instant coffee for the white chocolate.

coffee madeleines

ingredients

makes 12

1 large egg
50 g/1¾ oz caster sugar
1 tsp coffee and chicory essence
55 g/2 oz self-raising flour,
    plus extra for dusting
40 g/1½ oz butter, melted,
    plus extra for greasing

icing

85 g/3 oz icing sugar, sifted
4–5 tsp strong black coffee, cooled

method

1 Preheat the oven to 190°C/375°F/Gas Mark 5. Thoroughly grease a 12-hole madeleine tin with butter, then lightly dust with flour, tipping out any excess.

2 Put the egg, sugar and coffee and chicory essence into a heatproof bowl set over a saucepan of simmering water. Beat with an electric whisk until the mixture is thick and pale and leaves a trail on the surface when the whisk is lifted.

3 Sift in half the flour and fold in gently, then pour over half the butter and fold in until just incorporated. Repeat with the remaining flour and butter.

4 Spoon the mixture into the prepared tin, taking care not to overfill each hole. Bake in the preheated oven for 8–10 minutes, or until risen and springy to the touch. Leave in the tin for 5 minutes, then turn out onto a wire rack and leave to cool.

5 To make the icing, put the sugar and coffee in a small bowl and beat together until smooth. Dip each madeleine in the icing to coat just half. Leave to set on a wire rack.

marbled mocha whoopie pies

ingredients

makes 10

250 g/9 oz plain flour
1 tsp bicarbonate of soda
large pinch of salt
115 g/4 oz butter, softened
150 g/5½ oz caster sugar
1 large egg, beaten
150 ml/5 fl oz buttermilk
1 tsp vanilla extract
1 tsp strong black coffee, cooled,
    or coffee extract
1 tbsp cocoa powder

chocolate & cream filling

140 g/5 oz plain chocolate,
    finely chopped
450 ml/16 fl oz double cream
1 tbsp strong black coffee, cooled

method

1 Preheat the oven to 180°C/350°F/Gas Mark 4. Line 2–3 large baking sheets with baking paper. Sift together the plain flour, bicarbonate of soda and salt.

2 Put the butter and sugar in a bowl and beat with an electric whisk until pale and fluffy. Beat in the egg, then half the flour mixture and then the buttermilk. Stir in the rest of the flour, reserving 1 tablespoon. Transfer half the mixture to a second bowl. Stir the vanilla extract and remaining tablespoon of flour mixture into one bowl. Stir the coffee and cocoa powder into the second bowl. Swirl the two mixtures together to create a marbled effect.

3 Spoon 20 mounds of the mixture onto the baking sheets, spaced well apart. Bake in the preheated oven, one sheet at a time, for 10–12 minutes until risen and just firm to the touch. Cool for 5 minutes then transfer to a wire rack and leave to cool completely.

4 Put the chocolate in a heatproof bowl. Heat 200 ml/ 7 fl oz of the cream and the coffee in a saucepan until boiling then pour over the chocolate and stir until the chocolate has melted. Leave to cool for 20–30 minutes, stirring occasionally, until thickened. Whip the rest of the cream into firm peaks. Spread the chocolate mixture on the flat side of half of the cakes and top with the whipped cream. Top with the rest of the cakes

coffee cream macaroons

ingredients

makes 16

75 g/2¾ oz ground almonds
1 tsp coffee granules,
    finely crushed
115 g/4 oz icing sugar
2 large egg whites
50 g/1¾ oz caster sugar
1 tbsp amber sugar crystals,
    lightly crushed

filling

55 g/2 oz full-fat soft cheese
25 g/1 oz unsalted butter, softened
2 tsp strong black coffee, cooled
115 g/4 oz icing sugar, sifted

method

1 Put the ground almonds, coffee granules and icing sugar in a food processor or blender and process for 15 seconds. Sift the mixture into a bowl. Line two baking sheets with baking paper.

2 Put the egg whites in a large bowl and whisk until holding soft peaks. Gradually whisk in the caster sugar to make a firm, glossy meringue. Using a palette knife, fold the almond mixture into the meringue one-third at a time. Continue to cut and fold the mixture until it forms a shiny batter with a thick, ribbon-like consistency.

3 Pour the mixture into a piping bag fitted with a 1-cm/½-inch plain nozzle. Pipe 32 small rounds onto the prepared baking sheets. Tap the baking sheets firmly on a work surface to remove air bubbles. Sprinkle over the sugar crystals. Leave at room temperature for 30 minutes. Preheat the oven to 160°C/325°F/Gas Mark 3.

4 Bake in the preheated oven for 10–15 minutes. Cool for 10 minutes, then carefully peel the macaroons off the baking paper. Leave to cool completely.

5 To make the filling, place all the ingredients in a bowl and, using an electric whisk, beat until smooth. Use to sandwich pairs of macaroons together.

coffee cream & walnut cookies

ingredients

makes about 30

225 g/8 oz butter, softened
140 g/5 oz caster sugar
1 egg yolk, lightly beaten
2 tsp vanilla extract
225 g/8 oz plain flour
pinch of salt
55 g/2 oz ground walnuts
55 g/2 oz walnuts, finely chopped
sifted icing sugar, for dusting
    (optional)

coffee cream

85 g/3 oz butter, softened
140 g/5 oz icing sugar
1½ tsp strong black coffee, cooled

method

1 Put the butter and sugar in a large bowl and beat together until light and fluffy, then beat in the egg yolk and vanilla extract. Sift together the flour and salt into the mixture, add the ground walnuts and stir until combined. Halve the dough, shape into balls, wrap in clingfilm and chill in the refrigerator for 30–60 minutes.

2 Preheat the oven to 190°C/375°F/Gas Mark 5. Line two baking sheets with baking paper. Unwrap the dough and roll out between two sheets of baking paper. Cut out the cookies with a 6-cm/2½-inch fluted round cutter and place them on the baking sheets, spaced well apart.

3 Bake in the preheated oven for 10–15 minutes, or until light golden brown. Leave to cool on the baking sheets for 5–10 minutes, then transfer the cookies to wire racks to cool completely.

4 To make the coffee cream, put the butter and icing sugar in a bowl and beat together until smooth and thoroughly combined, then beat in the coffee. Sandwich the cookies together in pairs with the coffee cream, then press gently so that the cream oozes out of the sides. Smooth the sides with a dampened finger. Spread out the chopped walnuts in a shallow dish and roll the cookies in them to coat the sides of the coffee cream filling. Dust the tops with icing sugar, if liked.

mocha walnut cookies

ingredients

makes about 16

115 g/4 oz butter, softened,
plus extra for greasing
115 g/4 oz light muscovado sugar
85 g/3 oz caster sugar
1 tsp vanilla extract
1 tbsp instant coffee granules,
dissolved in 1 tbsp hot water
1 egg
175 g/6 oz plain flour
½ tsp baking powder
¼ tsp bicarbonate of soda
55 g/2 oz milk chocolate chips
55 g/2 oz walnut halves,
roughly chopped

method

1 Preheat the oven to 180°C/350°F/Gas Mark 4. Grease two large baking sheets.

2 Put the butter and sugars in a large bowl and beat together until light and fluffy. Put the vanilla extract, coffee and egg in a separate bowl and whisk together. Gradually add the coffee mixture to the butter and sugar, beating until fluffy. Sift the flour, baking powder and bicarbonate of soda into the mixture and fold in carefully. Fold in the chocolate chips and walnuts.

3 Spoon heaped teaspoons of the mixture onto the baking sheets, spaced well apart. Bake in the preheated oven for 10–15 minutes, or until crisp on the outside but soft inside. Leave the cookies to cool on the baking sheets for 2 minutes, then transfer to wire racks to cool completely.

peanut & coffee cookies

ingredients

makes 14

115 g/4 oz butter, softened,
 plus extra for greasing
115 g/4 oz soft light brown sugar
2 tsp coffee and chicory essence
1 tsp maple syrup or golden syrup
175 g/6 oz self-raising flour
75 g/2¾ oz unsalted, skinned
 peanuts, roughly chopped

method

1 Preheat the oven to 180°C/350°F/Gas Mark 4. Grease two large baking sheets.

2 Put the butter and sugar in a bowl and beat together until pale and creamy. Beat in the coffee and chicory essence and maple syrup. Sift in the flour, then add the peanuts and mix to form a rough dough.

3 Divide the dough into 14 even-sized balls and place on the prepared baking sheets, leaving plenty of room for the cookies to spread. Slightly flatten each ball with your fingertips.

4 Bake in the preheated oven for 12–14 minutes, or until just set and pale golden in colour. Leave to cool on the baking sheets for 5 minutes, then transfer to a wire rack to cool completely. The cookies will firm as they cool.

cappuccino cookies

ingredients

makes about 30

2 sachets instant cappuccino
1 tbsp hot water
225 g/8 oz butter, softened
140 g/5 oz caster sugar
1 egg yolk, lightly beaten
280 g/10 oz plain flour
pinch of salt

topping

175 g/6 oz white chocolate,
    broken into pieces
cocoa powder, for dusting

method

1 Empty the cappuccino sachets into a small bowl and stir in the hot, but not boiling, water to make a paste. Place the butter and sugar in a large bowl and beat together until light and fluffy, then beat in the egg yolk and cappuccino paste. Sift together the flour and salt into the mixture and stir until combined. Halve the dough, shape into balls, wrap in clingfilm and chill for 30–60 minutes.

2 Preheat the oven to 190°C/375°F/Gas Mark 5. Line two large baking sheets with baking paper. Then unwrap the dough and roll it out between two sheets of baking paper. Cut out cookies with a 6-cm/2½-inch round cutter and place them on the baking sheets, spaced well apart. Bake in the preheated oven for 10–12 minutes, or until golden brown. Leave to cool for 5–10 minutes, then transfer to wire racks to cool completely.

3 Place the wire racks over a sheet of baking paper. Put the chocolate in a heatproof bowl, set the bowl over a saucepan of gently simmering water and heat until melted. Leave to cool, then spoon the chocolate over the cookies. Leave the chocolate to set, then dust lightly with cocoa powder.

espresso sugar cookies

ingredients

makes 14

100 g/3½ oz butter, softened,
plus extra for greasing
55 g/2 oz caster sugar
1 tsp espresso coffee powder
115 g/4 oz plain flour,
plus extra for dusting
1 tbsp amber sugar crystals,
lightly crushed

method

1 Put the butter and sugar in a bowl and beat together until pale and fluffy. Beat in the coffee powder. Sift in the flour and mix to a soft dough. Gather the dough together with your hands and knead very gently on a lightly floured surface until smooth. Wrap in clingfilm and chill in the refrigerator for 1 hour.

2 Preheat the oven to 180°C/350°F/Gas Mark 4. Grease two baking sheets.

3 Roll out the dough on a lightly floured surface to a thickness of 5 mm/¼ inch. Use a 6-cm/2½-inch round fluted cutter to stamp out 14 rounds, re-rolling the dough as necessary. Place on the baking sheets. Sprinkle some sugar crystals in the centre of each cookie, pressing down gently.

4 Bake in the preheated oven for 10–14 minutes, or until the cookies are light golden around the edges. Leave to cool for 5 minutes, then transfer to a wire rack and leave to cool completely.

chocolate & coffee wholemeal cookies

ingredients

makes 24

175 g/6 oz butter,
    plus extra for greasing
200 g/7 oz soft light brown sugar
1 egg
70 g/2½ oz plain flour, plus extra
    for dusting (optional)
1 tsp bicarbonate of soda
pinch of salt
70 g/2½ oz wholemeal flour
1 tbsp bran
225 g/8 oz plain chocolate chips
185 g/6½ oz rolled oats
1 tbsp strong black coffee, cooled
100 g/3½ oz hazelnuts, toasted
    and roughly chopped

method

1 Preheat the oven to 190°C/375°F/Gas Mark 5. Grease two large baking sheets. Put the butter and sugar in a large bowl and beat together until light and fluffy. Add the egg and beat well. Sift together the plain flour, bicarbonate of soda and salt into another bowl, then add in the wholemeal flour and bran. Mix in the egg mixture, then stir in the chocolate chips, oats, coffee and hazelnuts and mix well.

2 Place 24 rounded tablespoons of the mixture on the baking sheets, spaced well apart. Alternatively, with lightly floured hands, break off pieces of the mixture and roll into balls (about 25 g/1 oz each), place on the baking sheets and flatten.

3 Bake in the preheated oven for 16–18 minutes, or until golden brown. Leave to cool for 5 minutes, then transfer to a wire rack to cool completely.

coffee & hazelnut biscotti

ingredients

makes 20

55 g/2 oz unsalted butter,
    plus extra for greasing
115 g/4 oz caster sugar
1 egg, beaten
55 g/2 oz mixed peel
55 g/2 oz blanched hazelnuts
2 tsp espresso coffee powder
½ tsp baking powder
175 g/6 oz plain flour

method

1 Preheat the oven to 180°C/350°F/Gas Mark 4. Grease a large baking sheet.

2 Put the butter and sugar in a large bowl and beat together until pale and creamy. Gradually beat in the egg, then stir in the mixed peel, hazelnuts and coffee.

3 Sift in the baking powder and flour and mix to a soft dough. Halve the dough and shape each piece into a 20-cm/8-inch x 10-cm/4-inch rectangle. Place on the prepared baking sheet.

4 Bake in the preheated oven for 20–25 minutes, or until just firm. Do not switch off the oven. Leave to cool on the baking sheet for 10 minutes, then, using a fish slice, transfer each rectangle to a chopping board and cut into 10 slices.

5 Place the slices cut-side down on the baking sheet. Return to the oven and bake for a further 8–10 minutes, or until golden and crisp. Transfer to a wire rack and leave to cool completely.

family cakes

mocha layer cake

ingredients

serves 8

butter, for greasing
200 g/7 oz self-raising flour
¼ tsp baking powder
4 tbsp cocoa powder
100 g/3½ oz caster sugar
2 eggs, beaten
2 tbsp golden syrup
150 ml/5 fl oz corn oil
150 ml/5 fl oz milk

filling

1 tsp instant coffee
1 tbsp boiling water
300 ml/10 fl oz double cream
2 tbsp icing sugar

to decorate

50 g/1¾ oz plain chocolate, grated
chocolate caraque
icing sugar, for dusting

method

1 Preheat the oven to 180°C/350°F/Gas Mark 4. Lightly grease 3 x 18-cm/7-inch shallow round cake tins. Sift the flour, baking powder and cocoa into a large bowl, then stir in the sugar. Make a well in the centre and stir in the eggs, syrup, corn oil and milk. Beat with a wooden spoon, gradually mixing in the dry ingredients to make a smooth mixture. Divide the mixture between the prepared tins.

2 Bake in the preheated oven for 35–45 minutes, or until springy to the touch. Cool in the tins for 5 minutes, then turn out and cool completely on a wire rack.

3 To make the filling, dissolve the instant coffee in the boiling water and put in a large bowl with the cream and icing sugar. Whip until the cream is just holding its shape, then use half the cream to sandwich the three cakes together. Spread the remaining cream over the top and sides of the cake. Press the grated chocolate into the cream round the edge of the cake.

4 Transfer the cake to a serving plate. Lay the chocolate caraque over the top of the cake. Cut a few thin strips of baking paper and place on top of the chocolate caraque. Dust lightly with icing sugar, then carefully remove the paper. Serve.

coffee & walnut ring

ingredients

serves 10

oil or melted butter,
    for greasing
175 g/6 oz plain white flour
1 tbsp baking powder
175 g/6 oz unsalted butter,
    softened
175 g/6 oz light muscovado sugar
3 eggs, beaten
1 tsp coffee extract
70 g/2½ oz walnuts, chopped,
    plus extra walnut halves
    to decorate
4 tbsp maple syrup

method

1 Preheat the oven to 160°C/325°F/Gas Mark 3. Grease a 1.5-litre/2¾-pint ring cake tin, preferably non-stick.

2 Sift the flour and baking powder into a large bowl and add the butter, sugar, eggs and coffee. Beat well until the mixture is smooth, then stir in the chopped walnuts.

3 Spoon the mixture into the prepared tin and smooth the surface with a palette knife. Bake in the preheated oven for 40–45 minutes, or until the cake is risen, firm and golden brown.

4 Leave to cool in the tin for 10 minutes, then turn out carefully onto a wire rack. While the cake is still warm, spoon over half the maple syrup. Leave to cool completely. To serve, top with walnut halves and drizzle over the remaining maple syrup.

gingerbread latte cake

ingredients

serves 10

175 g/6 oz butter,
  plus extra for greasing
150 g/5½ oz soft light brown
  sugar
115 g/4 oz golden syrup
115 g/4 oz treacle
2 tsp instant coffee granules
350 g/12 oz self-raising flour
2 tsp ground ginger
2 large eggs, beaten

frosting

125 g/4½ oz butter, softened
3 tbsp double cream
2 tsp coffee and chicory essence
225 g/8 oz icing sugar, sifted
1 tbsp demerara sugar
1 tsp instant coffee granules,
  finely ground

method

1 Preheat the oven to 160°C/325°F/Gas Mark 3. Grease a 20-cm/8-inch square cake tin and line with baking paper.

2 Put the butter, sugar, golden syrup, treacle and coffee granules in a small saucepan and heat gently until the butter has melted and the sugar has dissolved. Leave to cool for 10 minutes.

3 Sift together the flour and ginger into a large bowl. Stir in the melted mixture with the eggs and beat until smooth and creamy. Spoon the mixture into the tin and smooth the surface with a palette knife.

4 Bake in the preheated oven for 1 hour–1 hour 10 minutes, until the cake is risen, golden brown and a skewer inserted into the centre comes out clean. Leave to cool in the tin for 10 minutes, then turn out onto a wire rack to cool completely.

5 To make the frosting, put the butter into a bowl and beat with an electric whisk for 2–3 minutes, until pale and creamy. Beat in the cream and coffee and chicory essence, then gradually beat in the icing sugar and continue to beat for 2–3 minutes, until light and fluffy.

6 Swirl the frosting over the top of the cake. Mix together the demerara sugar and ground coffee and sprinkle over the frosting.

pecan coffee layer cake

ingredients

serves 10–12

280 g/10 oz self-raising flour
1 tsp baking powder
280 g/10 oz butter, softened,
    plus extra for greasing
280 g/10 oz caster sugar
5 eggs, beaten
1 tbsp instant coffee granules,
    dissolved in 2 tbsp hot water
70 g/2½ oz pecan nuts,
    finely ground
chopped pecan nuts, to decorate

frosting

450 g/1 lb full-fat soft cheese
2 tbsp maple syrup
115 g/4 oz icing sugar

method

1 Preheat the oven to 180°C/350°F/Gas Mark 4. Grease 3 x 23-cm/9-inch round sandwich tins and base-line with baking paper.

2 Sift together the flour and baking powder into a large bowl. Add the butter, sugar, eggs and coffee and beat with an electric whisk for 1–2 minutes, until creamy. Fold in the nuts.

3 Divide the mixture between the prepared tins and smooth the surfaces with a palette knife. Bake in the preheated oven for 20–25 minutes, until risen, golden and just firm to the touch. Leave the cakes to cool in the tins for 10 minutes, then turn out onto a wire rack to cool completely.

4 To make the frosting, put the cheese and maple syrup into a bowl and beat together until blended. Sift in the sugar and beat until smooth.

5 Sandwich the cakes together with one-third of the frosting. Spread the remainder over the top and sides of the cake and decorate with chopped pecan nuts.

coffee & walnut cake

ingredients

serves 8

175 g/6 oz unsalted butter, softened, plus extra for greasing
175 g/6 oz light muscovado sugar
3 large eggs, beaten
3 tbsp strong black coffee, cooled
175 g/6 oz self-raising flour
1½ tsp baking powder
115 g/4 oz walnut pieces
walnut halves, to decorate

frosting

115 g/4 oz unsalted butter, softened
200 g/7 oz icing sugar
1 tbsp strong black coffee, cooled
½ tsp vanilla extract

method

1 Preheat the oven to 180°C/350°F/Gas Mark 4. Grease 2 x 20-cm/8-inch round sandwich tins and line with baking paper.

2 Beat the butter and muscovado sugar together until pale and creamy. Gradually add the eggs, beating well after each addition. Beat in the coffee.

3 Sift the flour and baking powder into the mixture, then fold in lightly and evenly with a metal spoon. Fold in the walnut pieces. Divide the mixture between the prepared cake tins and smooth the surfaces with a palette knife. Bake in the preheated oven for 20–25 minutes, or until golden brown and springy to the touch. Turn out onto a wire rack to cool completely.

4 To make the frosting, beat together the butter, icing sugar, coffee and vanilla extract, mixing until smooth and creamy.

5 Use about half the mixture to sandwich the cakes together, then spread the remaining frosting on top of the cake and swirl with a palette knife. Decorate with walnut halves.

coffee bundt cake

ingredients

serves 14

400 g/14 oz plain flour,
    plus extra for dusting
1 tbsp baking powder
1 tsp bicarbonate of soda
3 tbsp espresso coffee powder
275 g/9¾ oz lightly salted butter,
    softened, plus extra for
    greasing
125 g/4½ oz light
    muscovado sugar
225 ml/8 fl oz maple syrup
3 eggs, beaten
225 ml/8 fl oz buttermilk
225 ml/8 fl oz double cream

to decorate

4 tbsp maple syrup
200 g/7 oz icing sugar
15 g/½ oz unsalted butter, melted
1½–2 tsp water
20 white and dark chocolate-
    coated coffee beans

method

1 Preheat the oven to 180°C/350°F/Gas Mark 4. Grease and lightly flour a 3-litre/5¼-pint bundt tin. Sift the flour, baking powder, bicarbonate of soda and coffee powder into a bowl. In a separate bowl, beat together the butter and muscovado sugar until pale and creamy. Gradually whisk in the maple syrup. Beat in the eggs slowly, adding 3 tablespoons of the flour mixture to prevent curdling.

2 Mix together the buttermilk and cream and add half to the butter mixture. Sprinkle in half of the flour mixture and fold gently together. Add the remaining buttermilk and flour mixtures and mix together until just combined.

3 Spoon the mixture into the prepared tin and smooth the surface. Bake in the preheated oven for about 50 minutes, or until well risen and a skewer inserted into the centre comes out clean. Leave in the tin for 10 minutes, then loosen with a knife and turn out onto a wire rack to cool completely.

4 Beat the maple syrup in a bowl with 150 g/5½ oz of the icing sugar and the butter, until smooth. Transfer the cake to a serving plate and spoon the icing around the top of the cake so it starts to run down the sides. Beat the remaining sugar in a bowl with the water to make a smooth paste. Drizzle the icing over the cake. Scatter the coffee beans over the top.

coffee fruit cake

ingredients

serves 10

300 g/10½ oz mixed dried fruit
150 g/5½ oz soft light
 brown sugar
150 g/5½ oz butter,
 plus extra for greasing
200 ml/7 fl oz strong
 black coffee
280 g/10 oz self-raising flour
2 tsp mixed spice
1 large egg, beaten
butter, to serve (optional)

method

1 Put the dried fruit, sugar, butter and coffee in a large saucepan and heat gently, stirring occasionally, until the butter has melted and the sugar has dissolved. Remove from the heat and leave to cool for 30 minutes.

2 Preheat the oven to 180°C/350°F/Gas Mark 4. Grease a 900-g/2-lb loaf tin and line the base and the two short sides with a strip of baking paper.

3 Sift together the flour and mixed spice into a large bowl. Make a well in the centre and pour in the fruit and coffee mixture and the beaten egg. Stir until thoroughly mixed.

4 Spoon the cake mixture into the prepared tin and level the surface. Bake in the preheated oven for 1 hour 15 minutes (covering loosely with foil after 50 minutes), or until the cake is firm to the touch and a skewer inserted into the centre comes out clean. Leave to cool in the tin for 10 minutes, then turn out onto a wire rack to cool completely. Serve sliced, spread with butter, if using.

mocha stollen

ingredients

serves 10

175 ml/6 fl oz milk
55 g/2 oz butter
2 tsp instant coffee granules
375 g/13 oz strong white flour,
    plus extra for dusting
25 g/1 oz soft light brown sugar
2 tsp easy-blend dried yeast
2 tsp mixed spice
¼ tsp salt
55 g/2 oz dried sweetened
    cranberries
40 g/1½ oz sultanas
25 g/1 oz mixed peel
1 egg, beaten
vegetable oil, for greasing
175 g/6 oz marzipan, rolled to a
    23-cm/9-inch sausage shape
icing sugar, to dust

icing

70 g/2½ oz icing sugar
2 tbsp cocoa powder
5–6 tsp milk

method

1 Put the milk, butter and coffee granules in a small saucepan and heat gently until the butter has melted. Leave to cool for 10 minutes.

2 Sift the flour into a large bowl and stir in the sugar, yeast, mixed spice, salt, cranberries, sultanas and mixed peel. Make a well in the centre and stir in the milk mixture and egg. Mix to a soft dough, then turn out onto a lightly floured surface and knead for 5–6 minutes, until smooth. Put in a bowl, cover with lightly oiled clingfilm and leave in a warm place for 1½ hours, or until doubled in size. Grease a large baking sheet.

3 Turn out the dough onto a lightly floured surface and lightly knead for 1 minute. Roll out to a 30-cm/12-inch long oval. Lay the marzipan down the middle of the dough and fold over the sides to enclose it. Place the stollen seam-side down on the prepared baking sheet. Cover with oiled clingfilm and leave in a warm place for 40–50 minutes, until doubled in size.

4 Meanwhile, preheat the oven to 190°C/375°F/Gas Mark 5. Bake the stollen in the preheated oven for 40–45 minutes, or until golden. Transfer to a wire rack and leave to cool. Sift together the sugar and cocoa powder into a bowl and stir in the milk. Drizzle over the stollen and leave to set, then dust with icing sugar.

raisin & cinnamon coffee crumb cake

ingredients

serves 10

175 g/6 oz butter, softened, plus extra for greasing
175 g/6 oz caster sugar
3 large eggs, beaten
3 tbsp strong black coffee, cooled
225 g/8 oz self-raising flour
2 tsp ground cinnamon
175 g/6 oz raisins
1 x 175-g/6-oz cooking apple, peeled, cored and finely chopped

crumb topping

85 g/3 oz self-raising flour
55 g/2 oz butter, chilled and diced
55 g/2 oz demerara sugar
2 tsp instant coffee granules, finely ground
40 g/1½ oz chopped mixed nuts
icing sugar, for dusting

method

1 Preheat the oven to 180°C/350°F/Gas Mark 4. Grease a 20-cm/8-inch round springform cake tin and base-line with baking paper.

2 Put the butter and sugar in a large bowl and beat together until pale and fluffy, then gradually beat in the eggs and coffee. Sift over the flour and cinnamon and fold in gently until thoroughly incorporated, then fold in the raisins. Spoon the mixture into the prepared tin and scatter over the chopped apple.

3 To make the topping, sift the flour into a bowl, then add the butter and rub in to make fine crumbs. Stir in the demerara sugar, coffee and nuts. Sprinkle the mixture evenly over the apple.

4 Bake in the preheated oven for 1–1¼ hours, until golden brown and firm to the touch and a skewer inserted into the centre comes out clean – cover loosely with foil after about 50 minutes if the crumb topping starts to over-brown. Leave to cool in the tin for 20 minutes, then unclip the tin and transfer the cake to a wire rack to cool completely. Lightly dust with icing sugar to serve.

banana mocha cake

ingredients

serves 10

1 tbsp instant coffee granules

2 tbsp water

200 g/7 oz soft light brown sugar

200 g/7 oz butter, softened, plus extra for greasing

3 large eggs, beaten

2 small bananas, peeled and mashed (about 150 g/5½ oz peeled weight)

225 g/8 oz self-raising flour, plus extra for dusting

frosting

85 g/3 oz plain chocolate, broken into pieces

15 g/½ oz unsalted butter

1 tbsp strong black coffee

method

1 Put the coffee, water and 2 tablespoons of the sugar in a small saucepan and heat gently, stirring, until the coffee and sugar have dissolved. Simmer for 1–2 minutes, until syrupy, then leave to cool.

2 Preheat the oven to 160°C/325°F/Gas Mark 3. Grease and lightly flour a 2-litre/3½-pint bundt tin.

3 Put the butter and remaining sugar in a large bowl and beat together until pale and fluffy. Gradually beat in the eggs, then the coffee syrup. Stir in the mashed banana, then sift in the flour and fold in thoroughly.

4 Spoon the mixture into the prepared tin and smooth the surface with a palette knife. Bake in the preheated oven for 45–50 minutes, or until the cake is firm and golden and a skewer inserted into the centre comes out clean. Leave to cool in the tin for 10 minutes, then turn out onto a wire rack to cool completely.

5 To make the frosting, put the chocolate, butter and coffee in a heatproof bowl set over a saucepan of simmering water and leave until melted. Remove from the heat and stir until smooth. Spoon the frosting over the top of the cake, gently easing it halfway down the sides. Leave to set.

espresso slab cake

ingredients

serves 12

3 tbsp cocoa powder
1 tbsp espresso coffee powder
4 tbsp boiling water
200 g/7 oz self-raising flour
1 tsp baking powder
175 g/6 oz butter, softened, plus
    extra for greasing
175 g/6 oz caster sugar
3 eggs
1 tsp vanilla extract
1 tbsp milk

frosting

200 g/7 oz mascarpone cheese
40 g/1½ oz caster sugar
1 tbsp espresso coffee, cooled
4 tbsp double cream
85 g/3 oz plain chocolate, melted

method

1 Preheat the oven to 180°C/350°F/Gas Mark 4. Grease an 18 x 28-cm/7 x 11-inch tray-bake tin and base-line with baking paper.

2 Put the cocoa powder, coffee powder and boiling water in a heatproof bowl and mix together to a smooth paste. Leave to cool for 10 minutes.

3 Sift together the flour and baking powder into a bowl and add the butter, sugar, eggs, vanilla extract, milk and cocoa mixture. Beat with an electric whisk for 2–3 minutes, until smooth and creamy.

4 Spoon the cake mixture into the prepared tin and smooth the surface with a palette knife. Bake in the preheated oven for 30–35 minutes, or until risen and just firm to the touch. Leave the cake to cool in the tin for 10 minutes, then turn out onto a wire rack to cool completely.

5 To make the frosting, put the mascarpone cheese, sugar, coffee and cream in a bowl and beat together until smooth. Spread over the top of the cake. Spoon the melted chocolate into a paper piping bag, snip off the end and pipe thin zig-zag lines across the frosting. Leave to set.

marble cake

ingredients

serves 10

55 g/2 oz plain chocolate, broken into pieces
1 tbsp strong black coffee
280 g/10 oz self-raising flour
1 tsp baking powder
225 g/8 oz butter, softened, plus extra for greasing
225 g/8 oz golden caster sugar
4 eggs, beaten
50 g/1¾ oz ground almonds
2 tbsp milk
1 tsp vanilla extract

icing

125 g/4½ oz plain chocolate, broken into pieces
2 tbsp butter
2 tbsp water

method

1 Preheat the oven to 180°C/350°F/Gas Mark 4. Grease a 1.7-litre/3-pint ring mould cake tin.

2 Put the chocolate and coffee in a heatproof bowl, set the bowl over a saucepan of gently simmering water and heat until melted. Leave to cool.

3 Sift the flour and baking powder into a bowl. Add the butter, sugar, eggs, ground almonds and milk. Beat well until smooth.

4 Transfer half of the mixture to a separate bowl and stir in the vanilla extract. Stir the cooled chocolate mixture into the other half of the mixture. Place spoonfuls of the two mixtures alternately into the prepared cake tin, then drag a skewer through to create a marbled effect. Smooth the surface with a palette knife.

5 Bake in the preheated oven for 50–60 minutes, until risen and a skewer inserted into the cake comes out clean. Leave in the tin for 5 minutes, then turn out onto a wire rack to cool.

6 To make the icing, put the chocolate, butter and water in a heatproof bowl, set the bowl over a saucepan of gently simmering water and heat until melted. Stir and pour over the cake, working quickly to coat the top and sides. Leave to set before serving.

spiced coffee & orange swirl cake

ingredients

serves 8–10

40 g/1½ oz pecan nuts
40 g/1½ oz soft light brown sugar
2 tsp mixed spice
1 tbsp instant coffee powder
225 g/8 oz self-raising flour
1 tsp baking powder
175 g/6 oz butter, softened,
    plus extra for greasing
175 g/6 oz caster sugar
3 large eggs, beaten
finely grated rind and juice
    of 1 orange

method

1 Preheat the oven to 180°C/350°F/Gas Mark 4. Grease a 20-cm/8-inch round cake tin and line with baking paper.

2 Put the nuts, brown sugar, mixed spice and coffee powder in a food processor or blender and process for a few seconds until finely ground.

3 Sift together the flour and baking powder into a large bowl. Add the butter, caster sugar, eggs and orange rind and juice and beat with an electric whisk for 1–2 minutes, until smooth and creamy.

4 Spread one-third of the cake mixture in the base of the prepared tin. Sprinkle over half the nut mixture. Repeat the layers once, then gently spread the remaining cake mixture on top. Drag a thin knife through the mixture to create a swirled effect.

5 Bake in the preheated oven for 55–65 minutes, or until risen and firm to the touch and a skewer inserted into the centre comes out clean. Leave to cool in the tin for 10 minutes, then turn out onto a wire rack to cool completely.

mocha-glazed pound cake

ingredients

serves 9

300 g/10½ oz plain flour
1 tsp baking powder
250 g/9 oz butter, softened,
    plus extra for greasing
225 g/8 oz caster sugar
1 tbsp coffee and chicory essence
6 eggs

mocha glaze

115 g/4 oz plain chocolate,
    finely chopped
1 tbsp coffee and chicory essence
15 g/½ oz unsalted butter
150 ml/5 fl oz double cream

method

1 Preheat the oven to 180°C/350°F/Gas Mark 4. Grease a 20-cm/8-inch square cake tin and line with baking paper. Sift together the flour and baking powder into a bowl and set aside.

2 Put the butter and sugar in a large bowl and beat with an electric whisk until pale and creamy. Beat in the coffee and chicory essence, then beat in the eggs, one at a time, adding a spoonful of the flour mixture after each egg. Fold in the remaining flour. Spoon the mixture into the prepared tin and smooth the surface with a palette knife.

3 Bake in the preheated oven for 50 minutes–1 hour, or until risen and golden brown and a skewer inserted into the centre comes out clean. Leave to cool in the tin for 10 minutes, then turn out onto a wire rack to cool completely.

4 To make the glaze, put the chocolate, coffee and chicory essence and butter in a heatproof bowl. Heat the cream until almost boiling, then pour into the bowl. Stir constantly until the chocolate has melted. Leave to cool and thicken for about 20 minutes, stirring occasionally. Pour the thick glaze over the cake, allowing it to spill down the sides. Leave in a cool place to set the glaze.

coffee & walnut roll

ingredients

serves 6-8

butter, for greasing
3 eggs
1 egg white
100 g/3½ oz caster sugar, plus
extra for sprinkling
1 teaspoon coffee extract
70 g/2½ oz plain flour, sifted
40 g/1½ oz walnuts, finely
chopped, plus extra to decorate

filling

175 ml/6 fl oz double cream
35 g/1¼ oz icing sugar, plus extra
for dusting
1 tbsp coffee liqueur

method

1 Preheat the oven to 200°C/400°F/Gas Mark 6. Grease a 33 x 23-cm/13 x 9-inch Swiss roll tin with butter and line with baking paper.

2 Put the eggs, egg white and sugar in a heatproof bowl over a pan of very hot water. Whisk with an electric mixer until pale and thick enough to leave a trail.

3 Whisk in the coffee extract, then lightly fold in the flour and the finely chopped walnuts with a metal spoon. Spoon the mixture into the prepared tin, spreading evenly. Bake in the preheated oven for 12–15 minutes, until golden brown and firm.

4 Sprinkle a sheet of baking paper with sugar. Turn out the sponge onto the paper and peel off the baking paper. Trim the edges. Quickly roll up the sponge from one short side, with the paper inside. Leave on a wire rack to cool completely.

5 To make the filling, put the cream, sugar and liqueur in a bowl and whisk until the mixture begins to hold its shape.

6 Carefully unroll the sponge, remove the paper and spread the cream filling over the cake. Roll up carefully. Serve the roll dusted with icing sugar and decorated with roughly chopped walnuts.

chocolate cake with coffee syrup

ingredients

serves 12

225 g/8 oz plain chocolate,
    broken into pieces
115 g/4 oz unsalted butter,
    plus extra for greasing
1 tbsp strong black coffee
4 large eggs
2 egg yolks
115 g/4 oz caster sugar
55 g/2 oz plain flour
2 tsp ground cinnamon
50 g/1¾ oz ground almonds
chocolate-covered coffee beans,
    to decorate

syrup

300 ml/10 fl oz strong black coffee
115 g/4 oz caster sugar
1 cinnamon stick

method

1 Preheat the oven to 190°C/375°F/Gas Mark 5. Grease a 20-cm/8-inch round cake tin and base-line with baking paper. Put the chocolate, butter and coffee in a heatproof bowl, set the bowl over a saucepan of gently simmering water and heat until melted. Stir to blend, then remove from the heat and cool slightly.

2 Put the whole eggs, egg yolks and sugar in a separate bowl and whisk together until thick and pale. Sift the flour and cinnamon over the egg mixture. Add the almonds and the chocolate mixture and fold in carefully. Spoon the mixture into the prepared tin and bake in the preheated oven for 35 minutes, or until a skewer inserted into the centre comes out clean. Cool slightly before turning out onto a serving plate.

3 Meanwhile, make the syrup. Place the coffee, sugar and cinnamon stick in a heavy-based saucepan and heat gently, stirring, until the sugar has dissolved. Increase the heat and boil for 5 minutes, or until reduced and thickened slightly. Keep warm. Pierce the surface of the cake with a cocktail stick, then drizzle over half the coffee syrup. Decorate with chocolate-covered coffee beans and serve, cut into wedges, with the remaining coffee syrup.

coffee streusel cake

ingredients

serves 8

275 g/9¾ oz plain flour
1 tbsp baking powder
75 g/2¾ oz caster sugar
150 ml/5 fl oz milk
2 eggs
100 g/3½ oz butter, melted and
     cooled, plus extra for greasing
2 tbsp instant coffee, mixed with
     1 tbsp boiling water
50 g/1¾ oz almonds, chopped
icing sugar, for dusting

topping

75 g/2¾ oz self-raising flour
75 g/2¾ oz demerara sugar
25 g/1 oz butter, diced
1 tsp mixed spice
1 tbsp water

method

1 Preheat the oven to 190°C/375°F/Gas Mark 5. Grease a 23-cm/9-inch loose-bottomed round cake tin and line with baking paper.

2 Sift the flour and baking powder together into a large mixing bowl, then stir in the caster sugar. In a separate bowl, whisk the milk, eggs, melted butter and coffee mixture together and pour onto the dry ingredients. Add the chopped almonds and mix lightly together. Spoon the mixture into the prepared tin.

3 To make the topping, mix the self-raising flour and demerara sugar together. Rub in the butter with your fingertips until the mixture resembles breadcrumbs. Sprinkle in the mixed spice and water and bring the mixture together into loose crumbs. Sprinkle the topping evenly over the surface of the cake mixture in the tin.

4 Bake in the preheated oven for about 1 hour, or until a skewer inserted into the centre comes out clean. If the topping starts to brown too quickly, cover loosely with foil. Leave to cool in the tin. Turn out, dust with icing sugar and serve.

sachertorte

ingredients

serves 10

175 g/6 oz plain chocolate,
broken into pieces
140 g/5 oz unsalted butter,
plus extra for greasing
140 g/5 oz caster sugar
6 eggs, separated
175 g/6 oz plain flour

icing

225 g/8 oz plain chocolate,
broken into pieces
5 tbsp strong black coffee
175 g/6 oz icing sugar
6 tbsp apricot jam, warmed

method

1 Preheat the oven to 150°C/300°F/Gas Mark 2. Grease and line a 23-cm/9-inch round springform cake tin.

2 Put the chocolate in a heatproof bowl, set the bowl over a saucepan of gently simmering water and heat until melted. In a separate bowl, beat the butter and 70 g/2½ oz of the sugar until pale and fluffy. Add the egg yolks and beat well. Add the chocolate in a thin stream, beating well. Sift in the flour and fold it into the mixture. In a separate bowl, whisk the egg whites until they stand in soft peaks. Add the remaining sugar and whisk until glossy. Fold half the egg white mixture into the chocolate mixture, then fold in the remainder.

3 Spoon into the tin and smooth the top. Bake in the preheated oven for 1–1¼ hours, until a skewer inserted into the centre comes out clean. Cool in the tin for 5 minutes, then transfer to a wire rack to cool completely.

4 To make the icing, melt 175 g/6 oz of the chocolate and beat in the coffee until smooth. Sift in the icing sugar and whisk. Halve the cake. Spread the jam over the cut surfaces and sandwich together. Invert the cake on a wire rack. Spoon the icing over the cake and spread to coat the top and sides. Leave to set for 5 minutes. Transfer to a serving plate and leave to set for at least 2 hours.

chocolate truffle torte

ingredients

serves 10

butter, for greasing
55 g/2 oz golden caster sugar
2 eggs
25 g/1 oz plain flour
25 g/1 oz cocoa powder,
    plus extra to decorate
50 ml/2 fl oz strong
    black coffee, cooled
2 tbsp brandy

topping

600 ml/1 pint whipping cream
425 g/15 oz plain chocolate,
    melted and cooled
icing sugar, to decorate

method

1 Preheat the oven to 220°C/425°F/Gas Mark 7. Grease a 23-cm/9-inch springform cake tin and base-line with baking paper. Place the sugar and eggs in a heatproof bowl and set over a pan of hot water. Whisk together until pale and mousse-like. Sift the flour and cocoa powder into a separate bowl, then fold gently into the cake mixture. Pour into the prepared tin and bake in the preheated oven for 7–10 minutes, or until risen and firm to the touch.

2 Transfer to a wire rack to cool. Wash and dry the tin and replace the cooled cake in the tin. Mix the coffee and brandy together and brush over the cake.

3 To make the topping, place the cream in a bowl and whip until very soft peaks form. Carefully fold in the cooled chocolate. Pour the chocolate mixture over the sponge and chill in the refrigerator for 4–5 hours, or until set.

4 To decorate the torte, sift cocoa powder over the top and remove carefully from the tin. Using strips of card or waxed paper as a mask, sift bands of icing sugar over the torte to create a striped pattern. To serve, cut into slices with a hot knife.

white chocolate coffee gateau

ingredients

serves 8–10

40 g/1½ oz unsalted butter,
    plus extra for greasing
85 g/3 oz white chocolate, broken
    into pieces
125 g/4½ oz caster sugar
4 large eggs, beaten
2 tbsp very strong black coffee
1 tsp vanilla extract
125 g/4½ oz plain flour
white chocolate curls,
    to decorate

frosting

175 g/6 oz white chocolate, broken
    into pieces
85 g/3 oz unsalted butter
125 g/4½ oz crème fraîche
125 g/4½ oz icing sugar, sifted
1 tbsp coffee liqueur or very
    strong black coffee

method

1 Preheat the oven to 180°C/350°F/Gas Mark 4. Grease 2 x 20-cm/8-inch sandwich tins and base-line with baking paper.

2 Put the butter and chocolate in a bowl set over a saucepan of hot water and leave on a very low heat until just melted. Stir, then remove from the heat.

3 Put the caster sugar, eggs, coffee and vanilla extract in a large bowl set over a saucepan of hot water and whisk hard with an electric whisk until the mixture is pale and thick. Remove from the heat, sift in the flour and fold in lightly. Fold in the butter and chocolate mixture, then divide the mixture between the prepared tins. Bake in the preheated oven for 25–30 minutes, until golden brown and springy to the touch. Leave to cool slightly, then turn out onto a wire rack to cool.

4 To make the frosting, put the chocolate and butter in a bowl set over a saucepan of hot water and heat gently until melted. Remove from the heat and stir in the crème fraîche, icing sugar and coffee liqueur. Chill, stirring occasionally, until the mixture becomes thick and glossy. Sandwich the cakes together with some of the frosting and spread the remainder over the top and sides, swirling with a palette knife. Arrange the white chocolate curls over the top and leave to set.

italian coffee gateau

ingredients

serves 8

4 large eggs
115 g/4 oz caster sugar
115 g/4 oz plain flour
40 g/1½ oz butter, melted and
    cooled, plus extra for greasing
40 g/1½ oz plain chocolate,
    finely grated
cocoa powder, for dusting

espresso syrup

125 ml/4 fl oz espresso coffee
50 g/1¾ oz icing sugar

frosting

225 g/8 oz mascarpone cheese
85 g/3 oz caster sugar
2 tbsp Marsala

method

1 Preheat the oven to 180°C/350°F/Gas Mark 4. Grease 2 x 20-cm/8-inch round sandwich tins and base-line with baking paper.

2 Put the eggs and sugar into a heatproof bowl set over a saucepan of simmering water. Beat with an electric whisk until the mixture is thick and pale and leaves a trail on the surface when the whisk is lifted. Sift in the flour and fold in gently. Pour the butter over the mixture in a thin stream and fold in until incorporated.

3 Divide the mixture between the tins and bake in the preheated oven for 20–25 minutes, until light golden and springy to the touch. Leave to cool in the tins for 5 minutes, then turn out onto a wire rack.

4 To make the syrup, put the coffee and sugar in a small saucepan and bring to the boil. Simmer for 3–4 minutes, until syrupy. Leave to cool for 10 minutes. Pierce the tops of the warm cakes all over with a skewer and spoon over the coffee syrup. Leave to cool completely.

5 To make the frosting, put all the ingredients into a bowl and beat together until smooth. Spread half the frosting over 1 cake and sprinkle over half the grated chocolate. Top with the second cake and swirl the frosting over the top. Dust with the cocoa powder and sprinkle over the chocolate.

mocha cake

ingredients

serves 12

225 g/8 oz self-raising flour
1 tsp baking powder
2 tbsp cocoa powder
225 g/8 oz butter, softened,
    plus extra for greasing
225 g/8 oz soft light brown sugar
4 large eggs, beaten
115 g/4 oz plain chocolate, melted
2 tbsp caster sugar
3 tbsp strong black coffee

frosting

85 g/3 oz unsalted butter, softened
250 g/9 oz mascarpone cheese
55 g/2 oz icing sugar
2 tbsp strong black coffee, cooled
cocoa powder, to dust
chocolate-coated coffee beans,
    to decorate

method

1 Preheat the oven to 180°C/350°F/Gas Mark 4. Grease 2 x 20-cm/8-inch sandwich tins and base-line with baking paper.

2 Sift together the flour, baking powder and cocoa powder into a large bowl. Add the butter, brown sugar and eggs and, using an electric hand-held whisk, beat together for 3–4 minutes, or until the mixture is very smooth and creamy. Fold in the melted chocolate.

3 Divide the mixture between the prepared cake tins and bake in the preheated oven for 25–30 minutes, or until risen and firm to the touch.

4 Put the caster sugar and black coffee in a small pan and heat gently for 1–2 minutes. Leave to cool for 10 minutes. Pierce the tops of the warm cakes all over with a skewer and spoon the coffee syrup over the cakes. Leave the cakes to cool completely in the tins.

5 To make the frosting, place the butter and mascarpone cheese in a bowl and beat together until well blended. Beat in the icing sugar and coffee until smooth.

6 Remove the cakes from the tins and sandwich together with half the frosting. Swirl the remaining frosting over the top of the cake. Dust with cocoa powder and decorate with chocolate-coated coffee beans.

coffee & amaretto cream cake

ingredients

serves 8

175 g/6 oz self-raising flour
1 tsp baking powder
175 g/6 oz butter, softened,
    plus extra for greasing
175 g/6 oz soft light brown sugar
3 eggs, beaten
3 tbsp strong black coffee, cooled
55 g/2 oz plain chocolate, melted,
    and 1 tbsp toasted flaked
    almonds, to decorate

filling

450 ml/16 fl oz double cream
2–3 tbsp amaretto

method

1 Preheat the oven to 180°C/350°F/Gas Mark 4. Grease
   2 x 20-cm/8-inch round sandwich tins and base-line
   with baking paper.

2 Sift together the flour and baking powder into a bowl
   and add the butter, sugar, eggs and coffee. Beat with
   an electric whisk for 1–2 minutes, until smooth and
   creamy. Divide the mixture between the prepared tins
   and smooth the surface with a palette knife.

3 Bake in the preheated oven for 25–30 minutes, or until
   golden brown and springy to the touch. Leave to cool
   in the tins for 5 minutes, then turn out onto a wire rack
   to cool completely.

4 To make the filling, put the cream into a bowl with the
   amaretto and whip until it holds soft peaks. Sandwich
   the cakes together with half the cream and spread the
   remainder over the top. Spoon the melted chocolate
   into a paper piping bag and snip off the end. Pipe
   swirls of chocolate on the top of the cake and scatter
   over the flaked almonds.

desserts & sweets

coffee ice cream

ingredients

serves 6

25 g/1 oz plain chocolate, plus extra to decorate
225 g/8 oz ricotta cheese
5 tbsp low-fat natural yogurt
70 g/2½ oz caster sugar
50 ml/2 fl oz strong black coffee, cooled
½ tsp ground cinnamon
dash of vanilla extract

method

1 Grate the chocolate and set aside. Put the ricotta cheese, yogurt and sugar in a food processor or blender and process until smooth. Transfer to a large bowl and beat in the coffee, cinnamon, vanilla extract and grated chocolate.

2 Spoon the mixture into a freezerproof container and freeze for 1½ hours, or until slushy. Remove from the freezer, turn into a bowl, and beat. Return to the container and freeze for 1½ hours.

3 Repeat this beating and freezing process twice more. Keep in the freezer until 15 minutes before serving, then transfer to the refrigerator to soften slightly before serving. Serve in scoops, decorated with a little grated chocolate.

cappuccino ice cream

ingredients

serves 4

150 ml/5 fl oz full-fat milk
600 ml/1 pint whipping cream
4 tbsp finely ground fresh coffee
3 large egg yolks
100 g/3½ oz caster sugar
cocoa powder, for dusting
chocolate-coated coffee beans,
    to decorate

method

1 Pour the milk and 450 ml/16 fl oz of the cream into a heavy-based saucepan, stir in the coffee and bring almost to the boil. Remove from the heat, infuse for 5 minutes, then strain through a paper filter or a sieve lined with muslin.

2 Put the egg yolks and sugar in a large bowl and whisk together until pale and the mixture leaves a trail when the whisk is lifted. Slowly add the milk mixture, stirring all the time with a wooden spoon. Strain the mixture into the rinsed-out pan or a double boiler and cook over low heat for 10–15 minutes, stirring all the time, until the mixture thickens enough to coat the back of the spoon. Do not let the mixture boil or it will curdle. Remove from the heat and cool for at least 1 hour, stirring from time to time to prevent a skin forming.

3 Churn the cold custard in an ice cream maker, following the manufacturer's instructions.

4 To serve, whip the remaining cream until it holds soft peaks. Scoop the ice cream into wide-brimmed coffee cups and smooth the tops. Spoon the whipped cream over the top of each and sprinkle with cocoa powder. Decorate with chocolate-coated coffee beans.

brown sugar mocha cream

ingredients

serves 4–6

300 ml/10 fl oz double cream
1 tsp vanilla extract
85 g/3 oz fresh wholemeal
    breadcrumbs
85 g/3 oz dark brown sugar
1 tbsp instant coffee granules
2 tbsp cocoa powder
grated chocolate, to decorate
    (optional)

method

1 Whip the cream and vanilla extract together in a large bowl until it is thick and holds soft peaks.

2 Mix the breadcrumbs, sugar, coffee and cocoa powder together in another large bowl and layer the dry mixture with the whipped cream in serving glasses, ending with whipped cream. Sprinkle with grated chocolate, if using.

3 Cover tightly and leave to chill in the refrigerator for several hours, or overnight.

cappuccino mousses

ingredients

serves 4

1 sheet leaf gelatine
2 tbsp instant coffee granules
4 tbsp water
75 g/2¾ oz caster sugar
400 ml/14 fl oz double cream
1 large egg white
1 tbsp finely grated milk chocolate
4 chocolate-coated coffee beans,
    to decorate

method

1 Soak the gelatine in a bowl of cold water for 5 minutes, until soft. Place the coffee granules, water and 40 g/1½ oz of the sugar into a small saucepan and heat gently until the coffee has dissolved.

2 Drain the softened gelatine, squeezing out any excess water and add to the hot coffee. Stir gently, until the gelatine has dissolved, then leave the mixture to cool for 20 minutes.

3 Pour the cream into a bowl and whip until it holds soft peaks. Remove 6 tablespoons of the cream and reserve for decoration. Gently fold the coffee mixture into the remaining cream.

4 Whisk the egg white in a clean, grease-free bowl until holding soft peaks then whisk in the remaining caster sugar. Fold into the coffee cream and divide the mixture between four dessert glasses. Spoon the reserved whipped cream on top of the mousses.

5 Chill in the refrigerator for 1–2 hours, or until set. Sprinkle with the grated chocolate and decorate each mousse with a chocolate-coated coffee bean.

white chocolate tiramisù

ingredients

serves 4

16 Italian sponge fingers
250 ml/9 fl oz strong black coffee,
  cooled
4 tbsp almond-flavoured liqueur,
  such as amaretto
250 g/9 oz mascarpone cheese
300 ml/10 fl oz double cream
3 tbsp caster sugar
125 g/4½ oz white chocolate,
  grated
4 tbsp toasted flaked almonds,
  to decorate

method

1 Break the sponge fingers into pieces and divide half of
  them equally between 4 serving glasses. Mix together
  the coffee and liqueur in a jug, then pour half over the
  sponge fingers in the glasses.

2 Beat the mascarpone, cream, sugar and 50 g/1¾ oz
  of the chocolate in a bowl. Spread half the mixture
  over the coffee-soaked sponge fingers, then arrange
  the remaining sponge fingers on top. Pour over the rest
  of the coffee mixture, then spread over the remaining
  cream mixture. Sprinkle with the remaining chocolate.

3 Cover with clingfilm and chill for at least 2 hours,
  or until required. Sprinkle over the flaked almonds
  before serving.

espresso crème brûlée

ingredients

serves 4

450 ml/16 fl oz double cream
1 tbsp instant espresso powder
4 large egg yolks
100 g/3½ oz caster sugar
2 tbsp coffee liqueur,
    such as Kahlúa
4 tbsp caster sugar, for glazing

method

1 Preheat the oven to 110°C/225°F/Gas Mark ¼ and put four shallow ovenproof porcelain dishes on a baking sheet.

2 Place the cream in a small pan over medium-high heat and heat until small bubbles appear around the edges. Mix in the espresso powder, stirring until it dissolves, then remove the pan from the heat and leave to stand until completely cool.

3 Lightly beat the egg yolks in a bowl, then add the sugar and continue beating until thick and creamy.

4 Reheat the cream over medium-high heat until small bubbles appear around the edges. Stir the hot cream into the egg-yolk mixture, beating constantly. Stir in the coffee liqueur. Divide the custard mixture between the dishes and bake for 35–40 minutes, or until the custard wobbles slightly when you shake the dishes.

5 Remove the custards from the oven and leave to cool completely. Cover with clingfilm and leave to chill in the refrigerator for at least 4 hours, but ideally overnight.

6 Just before you are ready to serve, sprinkle each custard with the sugar and put the dishes under a very hot preheated grill until the topping is golden and bubbling. Leave to cool for a few minutes before serving.

hot chocolate soufflé with coffee sabayon

ingredients

serves 4–6

3 tbsp cornflour
250 ml/9 fl oz milk
115 g/4 oz plain chocolate,
    broken into pieces
4 eggs, separated
55 g/2 oz caster sugar,
    plus extra for coating
butter, for greasing
icing sugar, for dusting

sabayon

2 eggs, beaten
3 egg yolks
85 g/3 oz caster sugar
4 tsp instant coffee granules
2 tbsp brandy

method

1 Preheat the oven to 190°C/375°F/Gas Mark 5. To make the soufflé, place the cornflour in a bowl. Add a little milk and stir until smooth. Pour the remaining milk into a heavy-based saucepan and add the chocolate. Heat gently until the chocolate has melted, then stir. Pour the chocolate milk onto the cornflour paste, stirring. Return to the pan and bring to the boil, stirring. Simmer for 1 minute. Remove from the heat and stir in the egg yolks, one at a time. Cover and cool slightly.

2 Place the egg whites in a large, clean bowl and whisk until soft peaks form. Gradually whisk in the caster sugar until stiff but not dry. Stir a little of the egg whites into the chocolate mixture, then carefully fold in the remainder. Pour into a greased 1-litre/1¾-pint soufflé dish coated with caster sugar, then bake in the preheated oven for 40 minutes, or until it is well risen and wobbles slightly when shaken.

3 Just before the soufflé is ready, make the coffee sabayon. Place all the ingredients in a heavy-based saucepan over a very low heat and cook, whisking constantly, until the mixture is thick and light. Dust a little icing sugar over the soufflé and serve immediately, with the sabayon.

irish cream cheesecake

ingredients

serves 8

vegetable oil, for oiling
175 g/6 oz chocolate chip cookies
55 g/2 oz unsalted butter
crème fraîche and fresh
    strawberries, to serve

filling

225 g/8 oz plain chocolate,
    broken into pieces
225 g/8 oz milk chocolate,
    broken into pieces
55 g/2 oz caster sugar
350 g/12 oz cream cheese
425 ml/15 fl oz double cream,
    lightly whipped
2 tbsp Irish cream liqueur
1 tbsp strong black coffee, cooled

method

1 Line the base of a 20-cm/8-inch round springform cake
  tin with baking paper and brush the sides with oil.
  Place the cookies in a polythene bag and crush with
  a rolling pin. Put the butter in a saucepan and heat
  gently until melted. Stir in the crushed cookies. Press
  into the base of the prepared cake tin and chill in the
  refrigerator for 1 hour.

2 Put the plain and milk chocolate into a heatproof bowl,
  set the bowl over a saucepan of gently simmering
  water and heat until melted. Leave to cool. Put the
  sugar and cream cheese in a bowl and beat together
  until smooth, then fold in the cream. Fold the melted
  chocolate into the cream cheese mixture, then stir in
  the liqueur and coffee.

3 Spoon into the cake tin and smooth the surface with
  a palette knife. Leave to chill in the refrigerator for
  2 hours, or until quite firm. Transfer to a serving plate
  and cut into slices. Serve with crème fraîche and sliced
  strawberries.

caramel coffee pavlova

ingredients

serves 10

4 large egg whites
225 g/8 oz caster sugar
1 tsp vanilla extract
1 tsp white wine vinegar
1 tsp cornflour
2 tsp instant coffee granules,
   finely ground
2 tbsp chopped hazelnuts

filling

450 ml/16 fl oz double cream
2 tsp coffee and chicory essence
6 tbsp dulce de leche
25 g/1 oz plain chocolate,
   finely grated

method

1 Preheat the oven to 140°C/275°F/Gas Mark 1. Line a large baking sheet with baking paper and mark with a 23-cm/9-inch circle.

2 Place the egg whites in a clean, grease-free bowl and whisk until they hold stiff peaks. Gradually whisk in the sugar, 1 tablespoon at a time, until all the sugar has been incorporated and the meringue is firm and glossy. Mix together the vanilla extract, vinegar and cornflour and fold into the meringue with the coffee granules.

3 Spoon the meringue into a round on the lined baking sheet. Make a dip in the centre and swirl and peak the meringue with the back of a spoon. Sprinkle over the chopped hazelnuts.

4 Bake in the preheated oven for 1–1¼ hours, or until crisp on the outside. Turn off the oven and leave the meringue to cool in the oven for at least 2 hours or overnight (don't worry if it cracks a little on cooling).

5 To make the filling, put the cream into a bowl with the coffee and chicory essence and whip until it holds soft peaks. Gently fold the dulce de leche through the cream to give a rippled effect. Spoon the cream on top of the meringue and sprinkle over the grated chocolate.

mocha creams

ingredients

serves 2–4

12 marshmallows
125 ml/4 fl oz strong black coffee
55 g/2 oz plain chocolate,
    finely chopped or grated
300 ml/10 fl oz double cream

method

1 Put the marshmallows in a saucepan with the coffee and half the chocolate. Heat gently until melted. Remove the pan from the heat and leave to cool.

2 Whip the cream in a large bowl until thick and holding soft peaks, then gently stir in the coffee mixture.

3 Spoon into 2–4 serving bowls or dishes and sprinkle with the remaining chocolate. Leave to chill in the refrigerator until ready to serve.

mocha fondue

ingredients

serves 4

250 g/9 oz plain chocolate
(at least 50% cocoa solids),
broken into small pieces
100 ml/3½ fl oz double cream
1 tbsp instant coffee granules
3 tbsp coffee-flavoured liqueur,
such as Kahlúa

for the dippers

small sweet biscuits,
such as amaretti
plain or coffee-flavoured marbled
cake or sponge cake,
cut into bite-sized pieces
whole seedless grapes
firm peaches or nectarines, stoned
and sliced

method

1 Arrange the dippers decoratively on a serving platter or individual serving plates and set aside.

2 Put the chocolate in a heatproof bowl and set the bowl over a saucepan of gently simmering water, ensuring that the bowl does not touch the water. Add the cream and coffee granules and heat, stirring, until melted and smooth. Remove from the heat and stir in the liqueur, then carefully pour the chocolate mixture into a warmed fondue pot.

3 Using protective gloves, transfer the fondue pot to a lit tabletop burner. To serve, allow your guests to spear the dippers onto fondue forks and dip them into the fondue.

mochachino brownies

ingredients

makes 8–9

115 g/4 oz unsalted butter, plus
    extra for greasing
115 g/4 oz plain chocolate, broken
    into pieces
2 tbsp strong black coffee
250 g/9 oz caster sugar
1/2 tsp ground cinnamon
3 eggs, beaten
85 g/3 oz plain flour
55 g/2 oz milk chocolate chips
55 g/2 oz toasted walnuts, skinned
    and chopped, plus extra
    to decorate

white mocha sauce

100 ml/3 1/2 fl oz double cream
85 g/3 oz white chocolate, broken
    into pieces
1 tbsp strong black coffee, cooled

method

1 Preheat the oven to 180°C/350°F/Gas Mark 4. Grease and line a 23-cm/9-inch square baking tin.

2 Place the butter, chocolate and coffee in a medium-sized saucepan over a low heat and stir until just melted and smooth. Cool slightly.

3 Whisk in the sugar, cinnamon and eggs. Beat in the flour, chocolate chips and walnuts. Pour the mixture into the prepared tin.

4 Bake in the oven for 30–35 minutes, until just firm but still moist inside. Cool in the tin then cut into squares or bars.

5 Meanwhile, make the sauce by placing all the ingredients in a small saucepan over a low heat, stirring occasionally, until melted and smooth.

6 Place the brownies on individual plates and spoon the warm sauce on top. Decorate with chopped walnuts and serve.

raspberry dessert cake

ingredients

serves 8–10

250 g/9 oz plain chocolate, broken into pieces
225 g/8 oz unsalted butter, plus extra for greasing
1 tbsp strong black coffee
5 eggs
100 g/3½ oz caster sugar
70 g/2½ oz plain flour
1 tsp ground cinnamon
175 g/6 oz fresh raspberries, plus extra to serve
icing sugar, for dusting
whipped cream, to serve

method

1 Preheat the oven to 160°C/325°F/Gas Mark 3. Grease a 23-cm/9-inch cake tin and base-line with baking paper. Put the chocolate, butter and coffee in a heatproof bowl, set the bowl over a pan of gently simmering water and heat until melted. Remove from the heat and stir, then leave to cool slightly.

2 Beat the eggs and sugar together in a separate bowl until pale and thick. Gently fold the chocolate mixture into the egg and sugar mixture.

3 Sift the flour and cinnamon into another bowl, then fold into the chocolate mixture. Pour into the prepared tin and sprinkle the raspberries evenly over the top.

4 Bake in the preheated oven for about 35–45 minutes, or until the cake is well risen and springy to the touch. Leave to cool in the tin for 15 minutes before turning out onto a large serving plate. Dust with icing sugar before serving with fresh raspberries and whipped cream.

mocha coconut clusters

ingredients

makes 30

115 g/4 oz milk chocolate,
    broken into small pieces
25 g/1 oz butter
1 tsp instant coffee granules
55 g/2 oz desiccated coconut

method

1 Line 2–3 baking sheets with baking paper. Put the chocolate and butter in a heatproof bowl, set the bowl over a saucepan of gently simmering water and heat, stirring, until melted and smooth. Remove the bowl from the heat.

2 Stir the coffee granules into the chocolate until dissolved, then stir in the coconut.

3 Put heaped teaspoons of the mixture on the prepared baking sheets, cover and chill in the refrigerator until set. To serve, put each cluster in a paper sweet case.

mocha pecan tartlets

ingredients

serves 4

115 g/4 oz plain flour,
plus extra for dusting
85 g/3 oz unsalted butter,
chilled and diced
2 tbsp icing sugar
1 egg yolk

filling

55 g/2 oz soft light brown sugar
55 g/2 oz butter
1½ tsp instant coffee granules
40 g/1½ oz plain chocolate,
finely chopped
3 tbsp maple syrup
2 tbsp golden syrup
2 large eggs, beaten
125 g/4½ oz pecan nuts
whipped cream, to serve

method

1 Put the flour, butter and icing sugar into a food processor or blender. Process for a few seconds to make fine crumbs. With the machine running, add the egg yolk and process until the mixture begins to bind together. Turn out onto a lightly floured surface and knead gently until smooth. Wrap in clingfilm and chill in the refrigerator for 30 minutes.

2 Preheat the oven to 190°C/375°F/Gas Mark 5. Divide the pastry into 4 pieces. Roll out on a lightly floured surface and use to line 4 x 10-cm/4-inch loose-based fluted tartlet tins. Prick the bases with a fork and chill for 1 hour. Place a baking sheet in the oven.

3 To make the filling, put the sugar, butter and coffee granules into a small saucepan and heat gently, stirring, until the sugar and coffee have dissolved. Remove from the heat, add the chocolate and stir until melted. Leave to cool for 5 minutes, then whisk in the maple syrup, golden syrup and eggs.

4 Chop two-thirds of the nuts and stir into the mixture. Divide the mixture between the pastry cases and top with the remaining nuts. Place the tartlets on the preheated baking sheet and bake for 20–25 minutes, or until the pastry is golden and the filling has just set. Serve warm or cold with cream.

hot espresso cakes

ingredients

serves 6

oil or melted butter, for greasing
175 g/6 oz plain flour
1 tbsp baking powder
1 tbsp cocoa powder
175 g/6 oz unsalted butter,
  softened
175 g/6 oz light muscovado sugar
3 eggs, beaten
1 tsp vanilla extract
3 tbsp strong espresso coffee,
  cooled
brown sugar crystals, to serve

sauce

1 tbsp cornflour
200 ml/7 fl oz strong espresso
  coffee
100 ml/3½ fl oz single cream
40 g/1½ oz light muscovado sugar

method

1 Preheat the oven to 180°C/350°F/Gas Mark 4. Grease and line an 18 x 28-cm/7 x 11-inch rectangular cake tin.

2 Sift the flour, baking powder and cocoa into a large bowl and add the butter, sugar, eggs and vanilla extract. Beat well until the mixture is smooth, then beat in the coffee.

3 Spoon the mixture into the prepared tin and smooth the surface with a palette knife. Bake in the preheated oven for 30–35 minutes, or until the cake is risen, firm and golden brown.

4 Meanwhile, mix the cornflour with 2 tablespoons of the coffee, then add to a saucepan with the remaining coffee, the cream and sugar. Heat gently, stirring, until boiling, then reduce the heat and stir for 2 minutes, or until slightly thickened.

5 Using a 9-cm/3½-inch plain biscuit cutter, stamp out six rounds from the cake (trimmings can be eaten cold). Place on warmed serving plates, spoon over the sauce and sprinkle each with a few sugar crystals.

espresso mint chocolate truffles

ingredients

makes 24

225 g/8 oz plain chocolate,
    broken into pieces
55 g/2 oz unsalted butter
150 ml/5 fl oz double cream
2 tbsp espresso coffee, cooled
few drops peppermint extract
1–2 tbsp cocoa powder

method

1 Put the chocolate and butter into a heatproof bowl, set the bowl over a saucepan of gently simmering water and heat until melted. Remove from the heat and stir until smooth. Leave to cool for 5 minutes.

2 Mix together the cream, coffee and peppermint extract and stir into the chocolate mixture. Cool for 20–30 minutes, stirring occasionally, then leave to chill in the refrigerator for 2–3 hours, until firm enough to shape.

3 Sift the cocoa powder onto a flat plate. Divide and shape the chocolate mixture into 24 truffles, rolling lightly between the palms of your hands. Roll each truffle in cocoa powder to coat. Chill in the refrigerator for 1–2 hours, until firm.

variation

For a delicious nutty coating, roll the truffles in 115 g/4 oz finely chopped walnuts, pecans or pistachios instead of cocoa powder.

savoury recipes

coffee-braised beef pot roast

ingredients

serves 4

1.25 kg/2 lb 12 oz beef brisket joint

15 g/½ oz butter

2 tbsp sunflower oil

2 onions, cut into wedges

280 g/10 oz carrots, cut into chunks

280 g/10 oz parsnips, cut into chunks

300 ml/10 fl oz strong black coffee

200 ml/7 fl oz beef stock

2 tbsp tomato purée

2 tbsp Worcestershire sauce

1 tbsp balsamic vinegar

few sprigs fresh thyme, plus extra to garnish

2 tbsp cornflour

2–3 tbsp water

salt and pepper

boiled potatoes, to serve

method

1 Preheat the oven to 160°C/325°F/Gas Mark 3. Season the beef with salt and pepper.

2 Heat half the butter and half the oil in a large frying pan. Add the beef and fry over a high heat for a few minutes, until brown all over. Transfer to a large casserole dish.

3 Add the remaining butter and oil to the pan, then add the onions, carrots and parsnips and fry for 5 minutes. Stir in the coffee, stock, tomato purée, Worcestershire sauce and vinegar and bring to the boil.

4 Spoon the vegetables and liquid around the beef. Lightly season with salt and pepper and add the thyme. Cover and cook in the preheated oven for 2¼ hours.

5 Remove the casserole from the oven. Blend the cornflour to a paste with the water and stir into the hot liquid. Return the casserole to the oven, cover and cook for a further 30–40 minutes, until the beef and vegetables are very tender and the liquid has thickened.

6 Remove the beef from the casserole and carve into thick slices. Divide the vegetables and gravy between 4 shallow serving bowls, top with the beef and garnish with thyme sprigs. Serve with boiled potatoes.

blackened coffee rib-eye steaks

ingredients

serves 2

2 tsp finely ground espresso coffee

2 tsp dried oregano

1 tsp soft light brown sugar

1 tsp pepper

½ tsp sea salt

2 rib-eye steaks, each about
    225 g/8 oz and about
    2.5 cm/1 inch thick (at
    room temperature)

1 tbsp olive oil

25 g/1 oz butter

rocket and watercress salad,
    to serve

fresh Parmesan cheese shavings,
    to garnish

method

1 Mix together the coffee, oregano, sugar, pepper and salt and spread on a shallow plate. Dip each side of the steaks in the mixture to coat.

2 Heat the oil and butter in a large, heavy-based frying pan until sizzling. Add the steaks and cook on each side for 2–3 minutes, until black on the outside for medium-rare. Increase the cooking time slightly for well done steaks.

3 Transfer the steaks to a warmed plate. Cover with foil and leave to rest in a warm place for 10 minutes.

4 To serve, slice each steak into 5–6 slices and place on warmed serving plates. Pour over any meat juices and serve with a rocket and watercress salad, garnished with Parmesan cheese shavings.

beef in coffee sauce

ingredients

serves 6

4 tbsp sunflower oil
1.3 kg/3 lb braising steak,
    cut into 2.5-cm/1-inch cubes
4 onions, sliced
1 garlic clove, finely chopped
5 tbsp plain flour
300 ml/10 fl oz red wine
pinch of dried oregano
1 small fresh rosemary sprig
500 ml/18 fl oz black coffee
salt and pepper
fresh marjoram sprigs, to garnish
mashed sweet potatoes, to serve

method

1 Heat the oil in a large, deep frying pan. Add the steak cubes and cook over a medium heat, stirring frequently, for 8–10 minutes, until evenly browned. Using a slotted spoon, transfer to an ovenproof casserole dish. Preheat the oven to 160°C/325°F/Gas Mark 3.

2 Add the onions and garlic to the frying pan, reduce the heat and cook, stirring occasionally, for 10 minutes, until softened and just beginning to colour. Stir in the flour and cook, stirring constantly, for 1 minute. Gradually stir in the wine, a little at a time. Add the oregano and rosemary, season to taste with salt and pepper, pour in the coffee and bring to the boil, stirring constantly.

3 Transfer the mixture to the casserole dish. Cover and cook in the preheated oven for 2–2¼ hours, until the meat is tender. Remove and discard the rosemary sprig. Taste and adjust the seasoning, adding salt and pepper if needed. Garnish with marjoram sprigs and serve immediately with mashed sweet potatoes.

cowboy coffee burgers

ingredients

serves 4

1 tbsp instant coffee granules,
   finely ground
2 tsp soft light brown sugar
1 tsp salt
1/4 tsp pepper
500 g/1 lb 2 oz fresh beef mince
1 small onion, grated
1 egg yolk
olive oil, for brushing

to serve

4 burger buns
4 tbsp mayonnaise
1 tsp smooth mustard
peppery salad leaves
4 beef tomato slices

method

1 Put the coffee, sugar, salt and pepper into a large bowl and mix together. Add the beef, onion and egg yolk and mix together with your hands until thoroughly combined. Divide the mixture into four portions and shape each portion into a burger.

2 Preheat a griddle pan or cast-iron frying pan. Lightly brush the burgers with oil and cook for 6–8 minutes on each side, or until cooked through. Alternatively, cook under a hot grill.

3 To serve, split and lightly toast the burger buns. Mix together the mayonnaise and mustard. Put some salad leaves, a tomato slice and a burger on top of four bun halves. Add a dollop of mustard mayonnaise and top with the remaining bun halves. Serve immediately.

coffee barbecue-glazed spare ribs

ingredients

serves 4

2 racks pork spare ribs,
  about 800 g/1 lb 12 oz each
3 tbsp instant coffee granules,
  dissolved in 6 tbsp hot water
6 tbsp tomato ketchup
2 tbsp vegetable oil
3 tbsp Worcestershire sauce
3 tbsp smooth mango chutney
salt and pepper
salad, to serve

method

1 Put the racks of ribs into a large saucepan and cover with water. Bring to the boil, skim off any scum from the surface, then simmer for 25 minutes.

2 Lift the ribs out of the water and place on a metal rack set over a large roasting tin. Preheat the oven to 190°C/375°F/Gas Mark 5.

3 Put the coffee, ketchup, oil, Worcestershire sauce and chutney into a bowl and mix together. Season to taste with salt and pepper.

4 Liberally brush the coffee glaze over the racks of ribs. Roast in the preheated oven for 45 minutes, basting occasionally, until the glaze is sticky and lightly charred in places and the ribs are tender. Serve immediately with salad.

coffee-glazed ham

ingredients

serves 10

2 kg/4 lb 8 oz gammon joint
1 onion, quartered
few black peppercorns
1 bay leaf
100 ml/3½ fl oz strong
    black coffee
100 g/3½ oz demerara sugar
5 tbsp clear honey
2 tbsp wholegrain mustard
1 tbsp white wine vinegar
bay leaves, to garnish

method

1 Put the gammon into a large, deep saucepan and cover with cold water. Add the onion, peppercorns and bay leaf and bring to the boil. Reduce the heat to simmering, cover and cook for 1½ hours. Top up with more boiling water if needed.

2 Meanwhile, put the coffee, sugar, honey, mustard and vinegar into a small saucepan. Bring to the boil, then simmer for 10–15 minutes, until syrupy. Set aside.

3 Remove the gammon from the liquid and leave to cool for 10 minutes, then cut away the skin, leaving a thin layer of fat. Score the fat into diamonds with the tip of a knife. Line a roasting tin with foil and place the joint in the tin. Preheat the oven to 180°C/350°F/Gas Mark 4.

4 Pour two-thirds of the coffee glaze over the gammon. Roast in the preheated oven for 25 minutes, then pour over the remaining glaze. Roast for a further 35–45 minutes, basting 2–3 times, until the glaze is dark golden and caramelized at the edges.

5 Cover the joint and leave to rest in a warm place for 15 minutes before carving. Pour all the juices from the lined roasting tin into a small jug. Serve the gammon with the juices and garnished with bay leaves.

coffee-crusted lamb steaks

ingredients

serves 2

3 garlic cloves, crushed
1 tbsp instant coffee granules
2 tsp pepper
½ tsp sea salt
2 thick lamb rump steaks,
    about 175 g/6 oz each
1 tbsp sunflower oil
mint sprigs, to garnish

to serve

sautéed or boiled new potatoes
freshly cooked peas and beans

method

1 Grind the crushed garlic, coffee, pepper and salt into a rough paste using a pestle and mortar. Spread the paste over both sides of each lamb rump steak. Place on a plate, cover and leave to marinate at room temperature for 1–2 hours.

2 Preheat the oven to 200°C/400°F/Gas Mark 6.

3 Heat the oil in a frying pan until almost smoking. Add the meat and sear in the hot oil, turning, until browned all over.

4 Transfer to a shallow roasting tin and cook in the preheated oven for 15–20 minutes, depending on the thickness of the steaks and how well done you would like the meat. Remove from the oven, cover with foil and leave to rest in a warm place for 10 minutes.

5 Thickly slice each steak and arrange on warmed serving plates. Garnish with mint and serve immediately with potatoes and freshly cooked peas and beans.

coffee-marinated chicken drumsticks

ingredients

serves 4

8 large chicken drumsticks
150 ml/5 fl oz strong
    black coffee, cooled
3 tbsp clear honey
3 tbsp sweet chilli sauce
1 tbsp dark soy sauce
salt and pepper
chips and tomatoes, to serve

method

1 Place the drumsticks in a shallow, non-metallic dish. Mix together the coffee, honey, chilli sauce and soy sauce and pour over the drumsticks.

2 Lightly season with salt and pepper to taste, cover and leave to marinate at room temperature for 1–2 hours.

3 Meanwhile, preheat the oven to 200°C/400°F/Gas Mark 6. Remove the drumsticks from the marinade and place in a roasting tin. Roast in the preheated oven for 20 minutes. Meanwhile, pour the marinade into a small saucepan, bring to the boil, then reduce the heat and simmer gently for 15 minutes, until syrupy.

4 Remove the tin from the oven and pour the hot marinade all over the drumsticks. Return to the oven and roast, basting occasionally, for a further 20–25 minutes, or until they are cooked through and golden brown. Serve hot or cold with chips and grilled vine tomatoes.

turkey stir-fry with spiced coffee glaze

ingredients

serves 4

400 g/14 oz turkey breast fillet,
    sliced into thin strips
1 tsp finely grated fresh ginger
2 garlic cloves, crushed
1 tsp five-spice paste
4 tsp sesame oil
4 tbsp strong black coffee, cooled
4 tbsp teriyaki sauce
2 tbsp clear honey
2 tbsp rice wine vinegar
2 tsp cornflour
6 spring onions,
    trimmed and sliced
1 red pepper,
    deseeded and thinly sliced
1 yellow pepper,
    deseeded and thinly sliced
salt and pepper
boiled egg noodles, to serve

method

1 Place the turkey in a shallow, non-metallic bowl and add the ginger, garlic, five-spice paste and half the oil. Stir well, then cover and leave to marinate at room temperature for 1 hour.

2 Mix together the coffee, teriyaki sauce, honey, vinegar and cornflour in a jug. Cover and set aside.

3 Heat the remaining oil in a large wok until almost smoking. Remove the turkey from the marinade, add to the wok and stir-fry over a high heat for 3–4 minutes, until brown. Add the spring onions, red pepper and yellow pepper and stir-fry for a further 1–2 minutes.

4 Pour in the coffee mixture and continue stir-frying for 1–2 minutes, until the sauce has thickened and coated the turkey and vegetables. Season to taste and serve with noodles.

chilli espresso rub

ingredients

makes about 5 tbsp

2 tbsp dark brown sugar
1 tbsp ground espresso coffee
1 tbsp ground coriander
2 tsp ground cumin
1 tsp ground ginger
1–2 tsp dried red chilli flakes
    or chilli powder
salt and pepper

method

1 Mix all the ingredients together in a small bowl until thoroughly combined.

2 Rub the mixture thoroughly into meat, poultry, fish or seafood up to 6 hours before cooking.

3 Put in a shallow dish, cover tightly and chill in the refrigerator until required.

chilli with coffee

ingredients

serves 4

1 tbsp olive oil
1 red onion, chopped
2 garlic cloves, chopped
500 g/1 lb 2 oz fresh beef mince
1½ tbsp hot chilli powder
½ tsp ground cumin
1 tsp dried oregano
200 ml/7 fl oz strong
    black coffee
400 g/14 oz canned
    chopped tomatoes
2 tbsp tomato purée
1 tsp sugar
210 g/7½ oz canned red kidney
    beans, drained and rinsed
salt and pepper

to serve

soured cream
chopped fresh green chilli
tortilla chips

method

1 Heat the oil in a large, deep frying pan, add the onion
   and garlic and fry for 5 minutes. Add the beef and fry
   over a high heat for 8–10 minutes, stirring frequently,
   until brown all over.

2 Stir in the chilli, cumin and oregano and cook for
   1 minute, then add the coffee, tomatoes, tomato purée
   and sugar. Season to taste with salt and pepper and stir.
   Add the beans and cook, uncovered, for a further
   10–15 minutes.

3 Spoon into warmed bowls, top with spoonfuls of
   soured cream and some chopped chilli and serve
   immediately with tortilla chips.

coffee & walnut bread

ingredients
makes 1 loaf

vegetable oil, for greasing
200 g/7 oz strong wholemeal flour,
    plus extra for dusting
225 g/8 oz strong white flour
1 tsp salt
1 tsp easy-blend dried yeast
85 g/3 oz walnut halves,
    roughly chopped
300 ml/10 fl oz lukewarm water
1 tbsp instant coffee granules
1 tbsp olive oil
1 tbsp clear honey

method

1 Grease a baking sheet. Put the wholemeal flour, white flour, salt, yeast and walnuts into a large bowl and mix together. Put the water, coffee, olive oil and honey into a separate bowl and mix together. Make a well in the centre of the flour mixture and pour in the liquid. Mix with a knife to make a soft sticky dough.

2 Turn out the dough onto a floured surface and knead for 5–7 minutes, until smooth and elastic. Put the dough into a bowl, cover with oiled clingfilm and leave in a warm place for about 1 hour, or until doubled in size.

3 Turn out the dough onto a floured surface and lightly knead for 1 minute. Shape into a 20-cm/8-inch long oval and place on the prepared baking sheet. Dust the top of the loaf with wholemeal flour and slash a curve along the top of the loaf (just off centre). Leave in a warm place for 40–50 minutes, or until doubled in size. Meanwhile, preheat the oven to 200°C/400°F/Gas Mark 6.

4 Bake in the preheated oven for 18–20 minutes, or until golden brown and the base sounds hollow when tapped with your knuckles. Transfer the bread to a wire rack to cool.

drinks

s'mores coffee & chocolate cup

ingredients

serves 4

600 ml/1 pint milk
125 ml/4 fl oz strong black coffee
225 g/8 oz milk chocolate or plain
    chocolate (or a mixture),
    finely chopped
24 pink and white marshmallows
1 tbsp ready-made chocolate
    sauce, warmed
2 tsp finely grated plain chocolate

method

1 Put the milk and coffee into a saucepan and heat over a medium heat, until almost boiling. Remove from the heat and stir in the chopped chocolate. Whisk briskly until the chocolate has melted.

2 Return to the heat and simmer gently for 1–2 minutes. Preheat the grill to high. Divide the hot chocolate between four coffee cups or mugs and top with the marshmallows. Place the cups under the preheated grill for about 1 minute, until the marshmallows begin to brown and melt.

3 Drizzle over the chocolate sauce and sprinkle with the grated chocolate. Serve immediately.

cinnamon mocha

ingredients

serves 6

250 g/9 oz milk chocolate,
    broken into pieces
175 ml/6 fl oz single cream
1 litre/1¾ pints freshly
    brewed coffee
1 tsp ground cinnamon,
    plus extra to decorate

to decorate

whipped cream
marbled chocolate caraque

method

1 Put the chocolate in a large heatproof bowl set over a saucepan of gently simmering water. Add the single cream and stir until the chocolate has melted and the mixture is smooth.

2 Pour in the coffee, add the cinnamon, and whisk until foamy. If serving hot, pour into six heatproof glasses or mugs, top with whipped cream, a sprinkling of cinnamon and the caraque, and serve immediately. If serving cold, remove the bowl from the heat and leave to cool, then chill in the refrigerator until required. Pour into six glasses or mugs, top with whipped cream, a sprinkling of cinnamon and the caraque, and serve.

mocha whip

ingredients

serves 2

200 ml/7 fl oz milk
50 ml/2 fl oz single cream
1 tbsp brown sugar
2 tbsp cocoa powder
1 tbsp coffee syrup or instant
    coffee powder
6 ice cubes

to serve
whipped cream
grated chocolate

method

1 Put the milk, single cream and sugar into a food processor or blender and process gently until combined.

2 Add the cocoa powder and coffee syrup or powder and process well, then add the ice cubes and process until smooth.

3 Divide the mixture between two glasses. Top with whipped cream, scatter over the grated chocolate and serve.

hot caramel latte

ingredients

serves 2

55 g/2 oz granulated sugar
6 tbsp water
300 ml/10 fl oz milk
100 ml/3½ fl oz hot
    espresso coffee

method

1 To make the caramel, put the sugar and 2 tablespoons of the water into a small, heavy-based saucepan. Heat gently until the sugar dissolves, then boil rapidly for 4–5 minutes, without stirring, until the mixture turns to a golden caramel.

2 Remove from the heat and very carefully pour in the remaining water. Stir until the caramel dissolves, then return the pan to the heat and simmer for a further 3–4 minutes, until syrupy.

3 Put the milk into a separate saucepan and heat over a medium heat, until almost boiling. Remove from the heat, pour in the coffee and almost all the caramel sauce and whisk together until frothy. Divide between two tall latte glasses.

4 Drizzle the remaining caramel sauce over the top and serve immediately.

variation

For a festive winter latte, substitute 2 tablespoons of gingerbread-flavoured syrup (available in some supermarkets and online) for the caramel. Omit steps 1, 2 and 4.

coconut coffee cocktail

ingredients

serves 1

1 tbsp coconut liqueur
1 tbsp coffee liqueur
1 tbsp brandy
225 ml/8 fl oz freshly brewed
   hot coffee
whipped cream, to decorate

method

1 Mix the liqueurs and brandy together in a heatproof
   glass or mug.

2 Pour in the fresh coffee and decorate by topping with a
   spoonful of whipped cream.

amaretto coffee

ingredients

serves 1

1 measure amaretto
sugar
225 ml/8 fl oz freshly made strong
    black coffee
1–2 tbsp double cream

method

1 Put the amaretto into a warmed heatproof glass and add sugar to taste.

2 Pour in the coffee and stir.

3 When the sugar has completely dissolved, pour in the cream very slowly over the back of a spoon so that it floats on top.

4 Don't stir – drink the coffee through the cream.

hungarian coffee

ingredients

serves 1

1 measure brandy
sugar
225 ml/8 fl oz freshly made strong
    black coffee
1 tbsp grated chocolate
whipped cream, to serve
cinnamon stick, to decorate

method

1 Put the brandy into a warmed heatproof glass and add sugar to taste.

2 Pour in the coffee and grated chocolate, and stir.

3 When the sugar has completely dissolved and the chocolate has melted, top with the whipped cream and decorate with the cinnamon stick.

4 Don't stir – drink the coffee through the cream.

irish coffee

ingredients

serves 1

1 measure Irish whiskey
sugar
225 ml/8 fl oz freshly made strong
  black coffee
2–4 tbsp double cream

method

1 Put the whiskey into a warmed heatproof glass and add sugar to taste.

2 Pour in the coffee and stir.

3 When the sugar has completely dissolved, pour in the cream very slowly over the back of a spoon so that it floats on top.

4 Don't stir – drink the coffee through the cream.

coffee hazelnut soda

ingredients

serves 2

3 tbsp instant coffee granules
225 ml/8 fl oz boiling water
125 ml/4 fl oz sparkling water
1 tbsp hazelnut syrup
2 tbsp brown sugar
6 ice cubes
slices of lime, to decorate

method

1 Make the instant coffee with the water, cool to room temperature, cover with clingfilm and chill in the refrigerator for 45 minutes.

2 Pour the mixture into a food processor or blender, add the sparkling water, hazelnut syrup and sugar, and process well. Add the ice cubes and process until smooth.

3 Divide the mixture between two glasses, decorate the rims with slices of fresh lime and serve.

rum espresso with whipped cream

ingredients

serves 4

150 ml/5 fl oz double cream
300 ml/10 fl oz hot espresso coffee
1 tbsp rum
2 tsp demerara sugar,
    plus extra for sprinkling

method

1 Pour the double cream into a bowl and whip until it
   holds soft peaks.

2 Mix together the coffee, rum and sugar in a jug and
   pour into four small heatproof glasses or coffee cups.

3 Gently drop spoonfuls of the cream into the coffee.
   Sprinkle with a little extra sugar and serve immediately.

coffee & cinnamon egg nog

ingredients

serves 4

450 ml/16 fl oz milk
150 ml/5 fl oz strong black coffee
1 cinnamon stick
2 large eggs
85 g/3 oz caster sugar
100 ml/3½ fl oz double cream
2 tsp ground cinnamon

method

1 Put the milk, coffee and cinnamon stick into a saucepan and heat over a medium heat until almost boiling. Leave to cool for 5 minutes, then remove and discard the cinnamon stick.

2 Put the eggs and sugar into a bowl and whisk together until pale and thick. Gradually whisk in the milk and coffee. Return to the pan and heat gently, stirring all the time, until just thickened. Leave to cool for 30 minutes.

3 Put the cream into a bowl and whip until it holds soft peaks. Gently fold the cream into the egg mixture. Divide between four glasses, sprinkle with cinnamon and serve immediately, or chill for 1–2 hours in the refrigerator before serving.

midnight cowboy

ingredients

serves 1

1 measure brandy
½ measure coffee liqueur
1 tbsp double cream, chilled
crushed ice
cola

method

1 Slowly blend together the brandy, coffee liqueur, cream and ice in a blender until frothy.

2 Pour into a chilled glass. Top up with cola.

fuzzy martini

ingredients

serves 1

2 measures vanilla vodka
½ measure coffee vodka
1 tsp peach schnapps
cracked ice cubes
peach slice, to decorate

method

1 Shake the vanilla vodka, coffee vodka, and peach schnapps over cracked ice until well chilled.

2 Strain into a chilled cocktail glass and decorate with the peach slice.

black russian

ingredients

serves 1

cracked ice cubes
2 measures vodka
1 measure coffee liqueur

method

1 Fill a lowball glass halfway with cracked ice.

2 Pour over the vodka and coffee liqueur and stir to mix.

iced coffee with cream

ingredients

serves 2

400 ml/14 fl oz boiling water
2 tbsp instant coffee powder
2 tbsp brown sugar
6 crushed ice cubes

to decorate
single cream
whole coffee beans

method

1 Use the water and coffee powder to brew some hot coffee, then let cool to room temperature. Transfer to a jug, cover with clingfilm, and leave to chill in the refrigerator for at least 45 minutes.

2 When the coffee has chilled, pour it into a food processor or blender. Add the sugar and process until well combined. Add the crushed ice cubes and process again until smooth.

3 Divide the mixture between two glasses. Float single cream on the top, decorate with the whole coffee beans, and serve.

sweet milk coffee

ingredients

serves 6

6 tbsp canned sweetened condensed milk, or to taste

6 hot double espressos or strong-brewed Thai coffees

ice cubes, to serve (optional)

method

1 Put a tablespoon of condensed milk (or more to taste) in each of the six cups. Pour a hot double shot of espresso into each cup and stir.

2 For iced coffee, half-fill six tall glasses with ice cubes. Pour one cup of stirred espresso and condensed milk over the ice in each glass.

banana & coffee milkshake

ingredients

serves 2

300 ml/10 fl oz milk
4 tbsp instant coffee powder
150 g/5½ oz vanilla ice cream
2 bananas, sliced and frozen

method

1 Pour the milk into a food processor or blender, add the coffee powder and process gently until combined. Add half of the ice cream and process gently, then add the remaining ice cream and process until well combined.

2 When the mixture is thoroughly blended, add the bananas and process until smooth.

3 Divide the mixture between two glasses and serve.

tex-mex coffee

ingredients

serves 1

1 tsp light muscovado sugar,
    or to taste
2 tbsp Kahlúa or Tia Maria
1 tbsp gold tequila
150 ml/5 fl oz hot black coffee
1–2 tbsp double cream
grated plain chocolate,
    to decorate

method

1 Place the sugar, Kahlúa and tequila in a warmed heatproof glass with a handle. Add the hot coffee and stir until the sugar has dissolved.

2 Hold a teaspoon, back uppermost, just touching the surface of the coffee. Carefully pour the cream over the back of the spoon so that it floats on the surface.

3 Sprinkle with grated chocolate and serve immediately.

espresso galliano

ingredients

serves 1

2 measures Galliano
sugar
150 ml/5 fl oz freshly made strong
   black coffee
splash orange or lemon juice
orange zest strip, to decorate

method

1 Put the Galliano into a warmed heatproof glass and
   add sugar to taste.

2 Pour in the coffee and orange juice and stir until the
   sugar has completely dissolved.

3 Decorate with the orange zest.

mocha milkshake

ingredients

serves 2

100 ml/3½ fl oz black coffee,
  cooled
1 tbsp caster sugar
150 ml/5 fl oz milk
5 large scoops chocolate ice cream
2 tbsp ready-made chocolate sauce
aerosol cream, to serve

method

1 Put the coffee, sugar and milk into a blender or food
  processor and process for a few seconds until frothy.
  Add the ice cream and blend for a further 30 seconds.

2 Put the chocolate sauce into a paper piping bag. Snip
  off the end and pipe half the sauce around the inside
  of two chilled, tall milkshake glasses.

3 Pour the milkshake into the glasses. Top with swirls of
  cream and drizzle over the remaining chocolate sauce.
  Serve immediately.

index